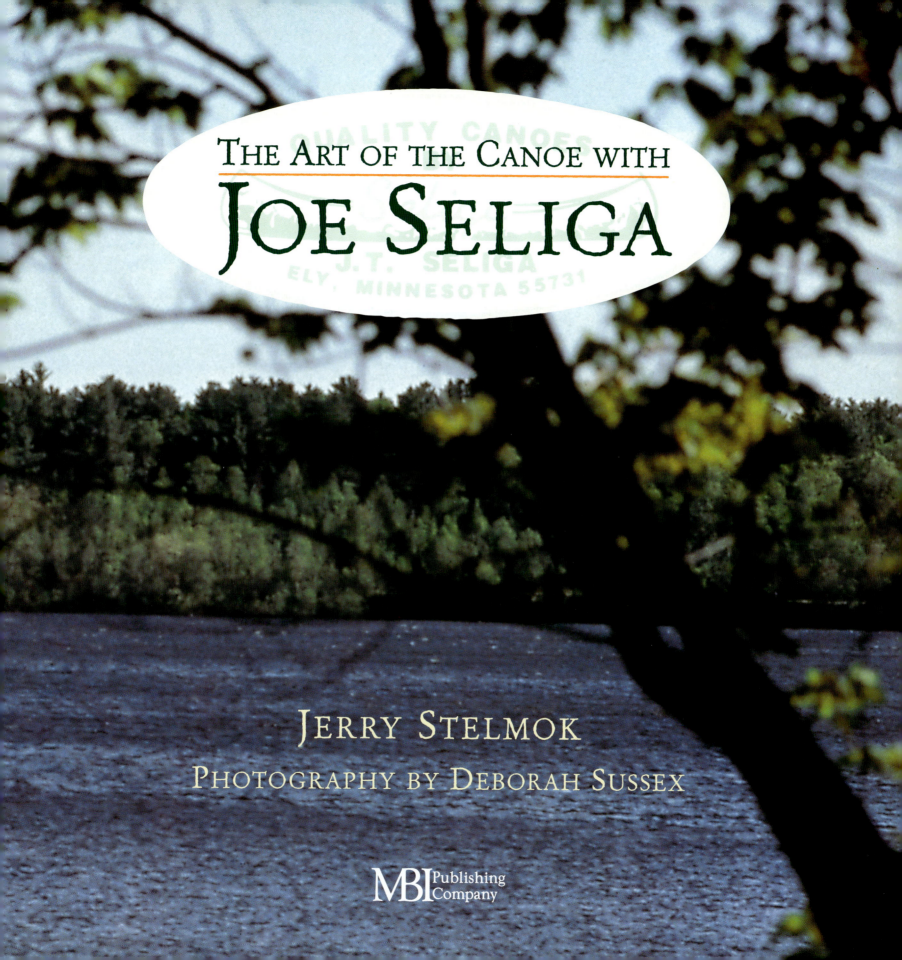

The Art of the Canoe with
Joe Seliga

Jerry Stelmok

Photography by Deborah Sussex

MBI Publishing Company

dedication

This book is dedicated to Eleanor "Nora" Seliga, my wife of 68-1/2 years,
whom I believe has driven more brass canoe tacks than any other woman, in addition to taking care of her family and home.
—Joe Seliga, 2002

Author's Acknowledgments

To borrow a phrase from John Donne, "No man is an island"—especially when he is compiling a book about a remarkable figure whose rich life and work now span nearly a century. Without the help, encouragement, and patience of dozens of individuals, the project would be like wrestling with an octopus, and the results would be as flat as a straw hat run over by a steamroller.

I owe the greatest debt of gratitude to Joe Seliga himself. A truly beautiful friend, whose good humor, patience, insight, and honesty went far beyond the boundaries of ordinary friendship to provide whatever I needed in the way of information, stories, family photographs, and of course, inspiration. Thank you, Joe. This thanks extends to Joe's family, who was always willing to provide information and photographs as soon as they were requested.

Another thank you goes to Joe's friend Dan Lindberg for generously allowing my use of his meticulously compiled record of Seliga canoes, which provided accurate and easily accessible information about Joe's canoe production all the way back to the beginning. I also wish to thank longtime friend Andrea Myers, whose computer skills, practiced eye, and great patience transformed my barely legible scratches on numerous legal pads into a readable and cyber-compatible manuscript.

I owe another debt of gratitude to "Jackpine" Bob Cary, not only for his illustration and introduction to the book, but also for the thoughts he freely shared about the town and neighbors he really cares about. Thanks also to Duluth columnist Sam Cook for gracing the book with his eloquent foreword. For information, stories, and impressions of Joe's canoes, I wish to thank Tom Kranz and Joe Smith at Camp Widjiwagan, as well as Chuck Rose and Allen Rench from the Charles Sommers Alumni Association, along with everyone who sent their memories of time spent in Seliga canoes. We could have filled up a second volume with all the great submissions. And thanks to friend, fellow canoe builder, and Ely resident Jeanne Bourquin for her hospitality, insight, and advice on numerous matters, and to Kerry Donars for a place to housesit while visiting Ely. And I mustn't forget the Iron Range Historical Society for providing the haunting image of the long-ago miners on page 11, or Sig's son Robert Olson of The Listening Point Foundation for providing the photo of his father.

Among knowledgeable friends here in Maine, who were kind enough to read over the material and offer comments and encouragement, I wish to cite and to thank northwoods guides Garrett and Alexandra Conover, as well as author and incomparable canoeing and hunting buddy Robert Kimber.

Also, it's rare to find an editor whose skill at his craft is matched by his genuine interest in the subject, but Iron Range native Dennis Pernu embodies these qualities, makes you take a hard look at the creation you are brewing, and, when necessary, perhaps saves you from yourself.

Of course, a tremendous thank you is extended to photographer Deborah Sussex, not only because her talent with a camera brings Joe's world to life, but for her support and professionalism throughout.

—*Jerry Stelmok*

Photographer's Acknowledgments

I feel honored to have had the opportunity to collaborate with Jerry and Joe on this project. I would like to thank Joe Seliga for inspiring me to be both thorough and exacting with my craft and to place the respect for people above all else. I appreciate Joe's consistent cooperation (and sense of humor) in allowing me to get in his way throughout many weeks of photographing. Additionally, I am grateful for the patience and support of Joe's family.

I also extend my thanks to Camp Widjiwagan. It was through my Widji experiences, opportunities, and friends that I felt such an important sense of belonging and focus in my teenage and young adult years. I will never cease to be amazed by how Widji has had a lifelong impact on my values, goals, and appreciation for the wilds.

Thanks to Jerry Stelmok for his knowledge and expertise of this subject. His guidance and support as a master builder himself helped me to best represent the fine details of canoe building. I also appreciate Jerry's thoughtfulness, his hard work, and of course, his sense of humor and ability to keep any situation on the fun side.

Thank you to MBI Publishing Company for the invitation to apply myself to what has been a very enjoyable project. Thank you to Dennis Pernu at MBI for his persistence, patience, creativity, and professionalism.

Finally, thank you to my husband Michael and my entire family for always encouraging me to dream big and follow my heart.
—*Deborah Sussex*

First published in 2002 by MBI Publishing Company, Galtier Plaza, Suite 200, 380 Jackson Street, St. Paul, MN 55101-3885 USA

© Jerry Stelmok and Deborah Sussex, 2002

All rights reserved. With the exception of quoting brief passages for the purposes of review, no part of this publication may be reproduced without prior written permission from the Publisher.

The information in this book is true and complete to the best of our knowledge. All recommendations are made without any guarantee on the part of the author or Publisher, who also disclaim any liability incurred in connection with the use of this data or specific details.

We recognize that some words, model names and designations, for example, mentioned herein are the property of the trademark holder. We use them for identification purposes only. This is not an official publication.

MBI Publishing Company books are also available at discounts in bulk quantity for industrial or sales-promotional use. For details write to Special Sales Manager at Motorbooks International Wholesalers & Distributors, Galtier Plaza, Suite 200, 380 Jackson Street, St. Paul, MN 55101-3885 USA.

Library of Congress Cataloging-in-Publication Data Available
ISBN 0-7603-1241-9

Edited by Dennis Pernu
Designed by Jerry Stenback

Front cover: Some of the 45 canoes Joe Seliga has built for Camp Widjiwagan since 1948 rest on the porch of the camp's well-appointed canoe shop, which will continue the master craftsman's legacy. The Nora and Joe Seliga Wood Canoe Endowment that was launched with the construction of the shop in 1998 has already met half of its $1 million goal.

Frontispiece: Joe's tray of brass canoe tacks also includes a 7-ounce ballpeen hammer, nail set, utility knife, block plane, homemade goring gauge, pencils, and a clinching iron Joe made himself.

Title Page: Master canoe builder Joe Seliga paddles one of his creations across Shagawa Lake near Ely, Minnesota, with author and fellow canoe builder Jerry Stelmok at the stern.

Back cover: **Top:** With all of the ribs for his latest canoe bent onto his form, Joe Seliga takes a moment to survey his work. In February 1994, a fire nearly destroyed Joe's backyard shop—the following spring and summer, a then 83-year-old Seliga replaced the charred rafters and rebuilt the roof, while wife Nora cleaned sooty brass fasteners with a toothbrush. **Bottom:** Joe and author Jerry Stelmok ply the waters of Shagawa Lake outside Ely, Minnesota, in one of Joe's canoes.

Printed in China

Contents

foreword
8

introduction
9

prologue
Ely, Minnesota: The North Country, Fair
10

chapter one
Coming of Age at the Edge of the Wilderness
22

chapter two
Lesson in Resourcefulness
35

chapter three
Recipe for the Good Life
51

chapter four
Camp Widjiwagan and the Seliga Legacy
70

chapter five
Building the Seliga Canoe
80

anatomy of a Seliga canoe
Art from the Northwoods
164

epilogue
The Magic Continues
166

index
168

Foreword

They are tucked away all over the north country. Hung carefully in garages. Resting on beams in boathouses. Stowed away in sheds. Seliga canoes. Elegant, practical canoes crafted by the hands of Joe and Nora Seliga. Seligas, with their gleaming ribs the color of honey. Seligas, with their perfectly upswept bows. Seligas, built for the rigors of travel in the Minnesota-Ontario border country.

And these gorgeous canoes are not found just in the canoe country. They've been tied on roof racks and hauled home to Illinois and Indiana and the East Coast, there to roost until those who own them make the pilgrimage back to Ely, back to the Boundary Waters Canoe Area, where a Seliga was meant to be paddled. And you can bet, every time those paddlers in far-flung reaches of the country go out to the garage to get in the car or retrieve a rake, they look up at their Seligas and almost hear the cry of a loon.

I do not know how many canoes Joe Seliga has built. That doesn't matter. It was never a numbers thing with Joe. It was a matter of getting the right materials and taking the time to build a boat he was satisfied to put his nameplate on. I can remember standing in his modest garage on Pattison Street in Ely, talking to Joe, with an almost-finished Seliga resting on carpeted sawhorses nearby. It might have just needed stem bands, or maybe a light sanding and another coat of varnish. You could almost imagine the person who had been waiting for that canoe. You could imagine how much it was going to mean the day that paddler drove north, walked in, and saw his finished craft. You could see him, running a hand over it, shooting the breeze with Joe, and finally driving off, the canoe lashed on top of his rig. That would be a good day.

One of my favorite memories of Joe is talking with him in his shop one morning. The sweet scent of cedar tickled my nostrils. The floor was splattered with every color Joe had ever painted a Seliga. As Joe talked, he leaned gently against one of his nearly completed canoes as it rested upright on the sawhorses. One arm was draped inside the canoe, and his weathered hand stroked the smooth finish along the curve of the ribs. He did this for several minutes, and I'm sure he was unaware of what he was doing. It reminded me of when I was a kid, and I used to idly toss a baseball into a well-seasoned mitt, just because it felt right. I imagine lots of places on a finished Seliga canoe—ribs, gunwales, bow deck, cane seats—have always felt right under the gentle touch of Joe's hands.

Many of those canoes have been handled just as lovingly by guides at the Sommers Canoe Base in Ely and at Camp Widjiwagan, where paddling a Seliga was a privilege to be earned. It says something not only about Joe Seliga but about the wood-and-canvas craft itself that so many of those canoes are still in use.

Something else needs to be said here, too. If you possessed the ability to build canoes as cherished as Seligas are, you wouldn't have to be nice. You could be a bit curmudgeonly or taciturn or vain, and people would still want your canoes. It happens, of course, that Joe is none of these things, that he is the nicest man you could ever hope to know. Fair. Modest. And a true woodsman.

You could easily imagine yourself paddling down a border-country lake with him, trolling a spoon for lake trout, out for a few days in the backcountry. He'd probably even let you carry the canoe over the portages—if you're careful.

—*Sam Cook*

Introduction

Step through the side door of a neat-appearing, cinder-block garage behind a two-story frame house on Pattison Street in Ely, Minnesota, and chances are you will first smell the aroma of white cedar sawdust. As your eyes grow accustomed to the reduced light, you may well see an ageless, friendly figure bent over the frame of a 17-foot canoe. As he has since 1938, Joe Seliga spends every spare moment in his shop, skillfully creating wood-and-canvas canoes.

Even at age 91, his sharp eyes and gnarled but nimble fingers bend on the ribs, lay up the planking, and tack on the fabric to complete one more of the more than 650 Seliga canoes that have gone out of Joe's shop and into the nearby Boundary Waters Canoe Area Wilderness—or perhaps across the country. And until her death in October 2000, Nora, Joe's loving wife of 68 years, could generally be found working alongside him.

Born and raised in Ely, son of middle-European immigrants, Joe found early on that survival on Minnesota's northern border meant working a shift in the dangerous confines of an underground iron mine, then supplementing that wage with whatever fish, game, berries, and wild rice could be garnered from the surrounding forests and lakes. Like the region's original Ojibwe residents, it did not take the Seliga family long to discover that the best hunting, fishing, and gathering was in the back country, accessible only by paddle. He got his first experience at canoe work while rebuilding the family canoe after an upset on the Nina Moose River. Painstakingly restoring cracked ribs and shattered planking, Joe studied the details of canoe construction, then set about building craft of his own.

His first canoes found a ready market among local paddlers, and with each sale Joe acquired the capital to build another. And another. An avid angler and hunter, he field-tested each design at night and on weekends, noting where improvements could be made. Eventually, he journeyed to Old Town, Maine, visiting the famed factory of the same name. Through discreet inquiry, Joe added to his store of knowledge.

Ely journalist, writer, and artist "Jackpine" Bob Cary rendered this drawing of Joe in the 1960s. *Joe Seliga Collection*

Joe allows that his legs and back will no longer withstand the rigors of wilderness portages, but he labors on in his garage. Occasionally, an old crony, veteran guide, or retired outfitter will drop by to swap a few yarns of the old days, a skill Joe handles without missing a single stroke of his hammer or swipe of his sandpaper block. No longer are Joe's craft commercial ventures. They have become collectors' items, superb hand-built examples of the old-time canoe-maker's skill, as much a piece of art as a Frederic Remington painting. Lucky, indeed, is the man or woman who owns a Seliga original. Luckier yet are those of us who have known him as a friend and have shared his good humor, his quiet optimism, and his vision of what lies just around the next bend in the river.

—*"Jackpine" Bob Cary*

Ely, Minnesota: The North Country, Fair

Joe Seliga surveys a recently completed canoe
from the doorway of his backyard shop in Ely, Minnesota.

Walking the streets of Ely, Minnesota, with Joe Seliga in late July 2001 is not unlike accompanying a favorite congressman or senator through a strong district—he thanks supporters and is recharged by continuous smiles and greetings from well-wishers. But Seliga is no politician, at least not in the official sense. He is a lifelong resident of the town, a former iron ore miner, and, for the past 64 years, a skilled and celebrated canoe builder. That is not a misprint: Joe Seliga turned 90 in April 2001, but he has the stamina and vitality of men 25 years his junior, and the features to match.

Ely miners, candlestick hats and all, are pictured at the Pioneer Mine near Ely in 1902.
Courtesy Iron Range Historical Society

Not only does Joe still have all of his straight brown hair, most of it has yet to turn gray. The wrinkles on his tanned face look like those of any outdoorsman and are no clear indicator of his years. Joe is a little below average in height and is neither overweight nor too thin. His eyes squint nearly shut in the bright sunlight, and even indoors they give this impression; but a dancing light sparkles between the lids, suggesting a luminous spirit back there, wide awake, taking everything in and emanating warmth and good humor. His thin mouth is set in a slight grin that broadens appreciably when he encounters friends and acquaintances, which seems about every half-block. It's a warm summer morning and Joe is wearing a crisp, short-sleeved checkered shirt, blue jeans rolled up a turn or two at the cuffs, and sneakers, further disguising his true age.

"There goes one," he says suddenly.

"One what?" I wonder, then follow his line of vision to where, a couple of blocks distant, a SUV with a green canoe on its roof turns the corner and disappears.

"Wonder who that could be?" he continues. "Probably an old 'Charlie.' Hard to tell."

Then I get it. Joe has spotted one of his canoes atop a car in the light traffic, 100 yards away just as it disappears down a side street. More remarkably, he fully expected to determine its vintage, if not its actual owner, despite the fact he has built over 650 of the craft over the years, and they have been dispersed to all corners of North America. A "Charlie" was a canoe guide at Northern Tier High Adventures, back in the days when it was known as the Charles L. Sommers Wilderness Canoe Base, a major purchaser of Seliga canoes. The fact that this sighting didn't result in a positive ID and a brief reunion is a little troubling to Seliga, but only for a moment. "Maybe he'll come by the shop this afternoon," he brightens.

His grin widens again as we turn into the Brandenburg Gallery, a tastefully appointed establishment that might have been dropped intact into this north-country town from Manhattan or Chicago's Michigan Avenue. Inside, neatly arranged on the white walls and under perfect lighting are the stunning works of local photographer Jim Brandenburg of *National Geographic* fame. A stylish woman in a long dress swishes up, plants a kiss on Joe's cheek, and squeezes him in a warm hug. Joe's grin gets even wider. "Gee, Millie," he jokes, "if I knew you missed me this much, I'd come by more often." It's the same everywhere we go: the women love Joe and he obviously enjoys the attention. Millie Bissonett, the gallery hostess, is an old friend, and her husband Barry is responsible for many of the impressive log buildings scattered around town and the shores of nearby lakes. Because he is always buying quality timber, Bissonett keeps an eye out for quality cedar and has provided Seliga with exceptional canoe stock.

Joe points out a poster with a brilliant image taken in autumn. The sky is cobalt blue, and the yellow and orange birch and tamaracks cast perfect reflections on the mirror surface of the water. The lower half of the idyllic image is split by the recurved bow of a Seliga canoe with a mahogany deck. The image is a familiar one, having been used by the state of Minnesota on posters, brochures, and coffee mugs to promote the border lakes country. The canoe in the photo belongs to Brandenburg. As we leave, Millie gives Joe another kiss and promises she'll ask her husband about a batch of logs they've been discussing.

Soon, we're seated in a corner booth at Britton's Café on Chapman Street. The restaurant is practically full and it's easy to see that most of the customers are Ely locals. No one's wearing khaki shorts with a half-dozen pockets and there are few polo shirts, Tilley hats, or hiking boots in evidence. A long counter stretching into the depths of the narrow dining room augments the seating capacity. Had Norman Rockwell set up his easel here, the resulting painting would not look out of place on the cover of a 1959 *Saturday Evening Post*.

A waitress with glasses and a ponytail spots Joe and rushes over with a friendly smile on her face and a coffeepot and two mugs in her hands.

"Joe," she lilts in thick Midwesternese. "I knew you'd be in today. You always know when we're having the meatloaf, don't you?" We could be in Lake Wobegon, but there is no radio crew.

"Oh, I know, all right," Joe chuckles. "You couldn't keep me away with a shotgun." He winks to me.

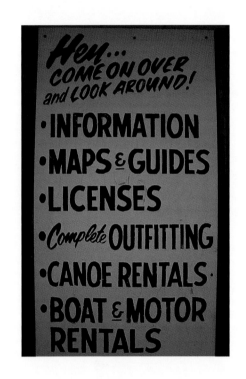

Decades of experience have turned local outfitters into one-stop service centers.

"We'd have saved you some anyway," she replies. "The meatloaf never goes to waste. Same for you, sir?" She nods toward me.

Of course. After all, this is not the kind of establishment where you order a tofu or nut burger. All of 5 minutes later, she sets down two heavy plates. "What took you so darn long?" Joe laughs. On each plate rests a thick slab of meatloaf, a fluffy mound of mashed potatoes swimming in rich, dark gravy, and green beans. Two huge white rolls with golden tops and butter sit on another plate. The food is steaming hot and delicious, and the chef was not bashful about adding enough salt to make it work. It's classic American diner fare at its best.

Joe's helping disappears without my noticing that he's eating. He's been talking about walleyes (which he loves), smallmouth bass (which he hates), canoes, and cedar, while greeting patrons as they arrive or depart. As the waitress refills our mugs, she reminds Joe that tapioca, another Seliga favorite, is on the dessert menu. Soon two dishes are set before us. I'd forgotten how perfectly this pudding tops off such a meal.

When we step out into the sweltering heat and bright sunlight, Joe blinks and shields his eyes for a minute. It's been an unusually long spell of steamy weather for this region, and I feel like I've eaten enough for a week. "Tell you what," Joe says. "Before we go back to the shop, let's swing by the IGA. They should have pasties today. I'd like to pick one up for dinner."

The typical visitor rolling into Ely, Minnesota, these days finds his or her way to this pleasantly isolated community for a taste of the northwoods, available in dainty sips as well as hearty draughts. Perched on the rim of the 1-million-acre Boundary Waters Canoe Area Wilderness (BWCAW), the town is the jumping-off point for thousands of canoeists each season eager to ply their blades in the clear, cold waters that fill countless lakes and ponds and run sparkling over scoured granite riverbeds. Here, where the soughing of wind through the red pines and jackpines replaces the familiar din of traffic, the stillness is disturbed infrequently and

This typical Ely outfitter is ready to provide the traveler with everything necessary to mount a trip into the Boundary Waters Canoe Area Wilderness.

often only by the evocative call of the loon or the distant, nighttime howling of a pack of wolves. And although any paddler here shares this paradise with hundreds of fellow adventurers on any given summertime week, the park is large and has enough campsites so that it is possible to enjoy a real sense of wilderness even during this busy season. Late spring or autumn sojourns afford an even greater opportunity to enjoy sections of the BWCAW, essentially to oneself.

But it's not only canoeists who pour into Ely in the summer. Dozens of resorts located on the edge of the wilderness area offer the chance to enjoy the natural beauty, pure water, and rugged scenery, or to pursue several species of abundant game fish without the planning, minor discomforts, and work inherent in wilderness camping.

The businesses of downtown Ely, poised largely along Sheridan Street, are stocked and ready to offer all comers whatever supplies are needed, or to take a bit of the northwoods experience back home with them. Canoe outfitting operations, many in the business for decades, provide everything from canoes and transportation to starting points, tents, PFDs, cooking kits, fishing tackle, clothing, sleeping bags, and assistance in obtaining the required entry permits.

There is a restaurant or café for every taste and budget, and the common flavor is casual and friendly. There are saloons mainly serving

The headframe and water tower over the old Pioneer shaft, which has been capped. The Trezona Trail encircles Miner's Lake, providing a popular walking, biking, and skiing path close to town.

draft beer to fisherman, hunters, and snowmobilers, and others serving these same patrons alongside scotch- and wine-sipping ecotourists more interested in the latest novel than the largest walleye caught that week.

Those who aim to find the perfect souvenir or just enjoy shopping are not disappointed either. Along with vendors of clever T-shirts, moose and wolf bric-a-brac, and loon motifs of every description, there are others specializing in unique, well-crafted cottage furnishings, beautifully designed and locally made outdoor clothing, books, and artwork.

This resort community atmosphere, reminiscent of that along the East Coast or in New York's Adirondack Park, was not Ely's original flavor. It reflects a determined and creative redirection of the town's energy in regard to the natural resources around it: a shift from the extractive industries of iron mining and logging to more sustainable businesses based on the recreational opportunities afforded by the wilderness of the surrounding region. This new direction has been built on the shoulders of the sport fishery, canoe livery, and summer camp establishments that have thrived in and about Ely for generations—and accelerated by the demise of logging and the collapse of the mining operations. The restructuring is a change that does not meet the unqualified approval of all longtime residents, many of whom long for a return to simpler times under the care—and in the control of—mining interests.

Minnesota's Iron Range extends across the eastern third of the state's northern reaches. Part of the Laurentian Divide, which separates north and south watersheds, the Iron Range holds extremely pure veins of iron ore that stretch fingers north between the myriad border lakes and fall off toward the farming country to the southwest and the shore of Lake Superior to the east. The northern portion of the range is referred to as the Vermilion Range and the southwest region as the Mesabi Range.

In the 1880s, a body of iron ore discovered in the wilderness south of Shagawa Lake near the present site of Ely would transform the pristine area into a booming mining center. Not only was the vein deep running and about a mile square in area, but its iron content was an incredible 60 percent. Additionally, the ore was rich in oxygen, making it ideal as a flux for purifying less-rich ore in the steel-making process.

In 1888, a rail line was punched in from nearby Tower and a number of mines began as surface operations, but were soon transformed into shafts, following the richest veins into the bowels of the earth.

Hundreds of jobs were created almost overnight, as men extracted the ore with pick, shovel, and dynamite, and cut timber to reinforce the shafts—and to build the town of Ely. The work was hard and conditions rough. European immigrants, largely single males or those with families left behind, arrived in droves and gave Ely, then called Florence, a reputation as a rough-and-tumble community, rich in saloons and brothels and lean in establishments like schools and

The striking interior of the Steger Mukluk retail store demonstrates the direction many Ely merchants are following to present quality, locally made products to increasing numbers of shoppers.

churches. Among the first job-seekers to bring along his family was Michel Seliga, who, in 1890, the year Ely was incorporated, arrived at the community of rough-board and log buildings with his wife and son, a strong back, and determination.

Within a few years, a half-dozen shafts were sunk into the earth just outside town. Production was phenomenal. Because of the ore's purity, there began in 1912 a 50-year period during which every batch of steel produced in the United States contained some percentage of Ely iron. During the peak production years just prior to the Great Depression, as many as 1,500 men were employed at the mines, among them Michel Seliga at the Chandler Mine, his son—and Joe's father—Stephen, at the Pioneer operation, and, beginning in 1941, Joe, at Zenith Mining.

Unlike most other boomtowns, Ely's source of wealth did not disappear overnight. And although the economy was not immune to the effects of recessions and depressions, for the better part of 80 years there a central unflagging engine existed behind a modest prosperity on which a diverse American town could sustain itself and grow. But it could not last forever, and on April 1, 1967, the Pioneer Mine, with a shaft 1,800 feet into the earth, ceased operation. Mining at that depth had become prohibitively expensive and new technology eliminated the requirement for high-oxygen iron in steel making. Over the previous 5 years, other mines in Tower and Ely had closed, and with the closing of the prolific Pioneer, the town's last 450 miners were faced with tough choices: retire early, commute to taconite operations in Babbit, relocate, or find another way to earn a living in the northwoods community that had become home.

Today, the largest physical evidence of Ely's mining past is a long thin body of water a mile and a half long, stretched between the south shore of Shagawa Lake and the town itself. Called Miner's Lake, it was formed when the abandoned shafts caved in one after another and filled with water. It is not a bad lake to look at and, not surprisingly, deep enough to support a healthy population of rainbow trout. The Trezona Trail around Miner's Lake is today popular with local hikers and cross-country skiers. From the steep bank above the lake's north shore, the impressive head frame and water tower of the Pioneer's "A shaft" stands vigil over the capped mine—the last man-made survivor of a robust time, and an impressive, if forlorn, reminder of the sweat, muscle, blood, and ingenuity required to dig and lift enough raw ore from the ground to build a city.

Ely's painful but successful transformation from mining to recreation and ecotourism is nowhere better highlighted than in two annual events

Each year, the snow sculptures crafted during Ely's Voyageur Winter Carnival become more detailed. This creative piece stands in front of the Chocolate Moose restaurant.

that together draw thousands of participants during the opposing seasons of high summer and deep winter. In late July or early August, the Blueberry Arts Festival brings hundreds of serious craftspersons to expansive Whiteside Park to hawk their creations to 40,000 or so attendees over three days. The fairgoers are treated to live music performances in the unique log pavilion and fed blueberry pancakes by the local Kiwanis—and just about every other variety of ethnic and carnival food by a squadron of vendors entrenched along the park's western border.

The winter counterpart to the Blueberry Festival runs a full week in early February (with a weekend at both ends) and provides a central event to bolster the community's ever-growing number of wintertime tourists: souls who brave possibly gruesome driving conditions, blowing snow, and sub-zero temperatures. Organized events include a snow-sculpture contest, concerts, cross-country ski and snowshoe races, dogsled rides, art exhibits, and the popular "Mukluk Ball." Like the Blueberry Festival, the Voyageur Winter Festival grows each year and helps jack up the spirits of the local residents who still face up to two more months of serious winter.

Many visitors to the region eagerly join residents in tuning in to the town's community radio station. WELY's "End of the Road Radio" is another established, local fixture, providing not only local news, but also an eclectic variety of blues, jazz, folk, bluegrass, and reggae. Items of local interest, like bear sightings, fishing hot spots, and reports from popular eateries, keep listeners informed on daily specials and fresh desserts. There is even a service where messages from isolated cabins with only CB radios can be broadcast to concerned parties, e.g., "Kate, Bill at Crawfish Point has the fish, please bring the corn!" In an age of cellular phones, this service seems to be more for fun than real necessity. Roving commentator Charles Kuralt fell in love with Ely his first time through and returned often. He purchased WELY in 1995, owning it until his death in 1997.

Bob Cary, senior editor at *The Echo*, one of the town's two newspapers, has been an Ely resident since the mid 1960s, and has an interesting perspective on life here.

Sitting at a booth in the Northern Grounds Café, a deli-style bakery and luncheon establishment, "Jackpine" Bob is radiant and animated as he talks about his adopted town. He appears much younger than his 80 years, even with his closely cropped white hair. What few wrinkles score his visage are clearly the work of wind and sunlight, not worry. It is easy to believe he is a former Marine who served in the South Pacific during World War II. His trademark fedora rests on the table and his reading glasses are either on the tip of his nose or in his hand.

Thirty-five years ago, Cary left what would seem to many a near-perfect job as outdoor editor of the *Chicago Daily News*. The position paid well and got him out in the woods and on the water with fellow sportsmen, often in regions that were Meccas for anglers and hunters. The hell of it was returning each time to the city and to his office. In 1966, he decided he'd had enough and fled to the region he loved above all others. Cary was not without the skills necessary to make a living in northern Minnesota. After the war, he had used the G.I. Bill to attend the Chicago Academy of Fine Arts, and used his talent as an artist to supplement his writing for local newspapers. Cary also had several contacts with outdoor-related interests, whom he used to establish Canadian Border Outfitters, the outfitting and guiding business he ran until 1973.

Writing articles and seven books, painting, and illustrating have supplemented his job as editor of the *Echo*, which is part-time these days. Never one to back down from a fight, he is well known locally for taking on the city council or anyone else on principles he believes in. A gallery upstairs at the café features Jackpine Bob's ink drawings and paintings, mostly outdoor and sporting scenes from all periods of his career. It's easy to recognize the work of a professionally trained artist with a good measure of talent.

Cary's wife Edie, a few years his junior (both have lost their first spouses), enjoys many of the same pastimes as Bob. Both are active cross-country skiers—including racing—with no plans to retire from the sport. And, yes, that was Bob I saw on stage with the Starlighters at the Blueberry Festival—with a straw hat and a set of snare drums.

Cary's pride shows when he talks about how Ely pulled itself up by its bootstraps after the demise of mining and a plunge in population from nearly 7,000 to just over 3,000—it is now back up to around 4,000 souls. There were great real estate bargains for awhile, he says, but that's surely changed, and people are again moving to the area, not a few of them for their retirements. There is also a boom in vacation-home-building, which provides projects for local contractors, helps the tax base, and doesn't add to the load of school children.

Cary is also quick to recognize the influx of talented "young" people who continue to relocate in the greater Ely region, bringing with them energy, new ideas, talent, and personal industry. Truly, there seems to be something in the air here that attracts gifted individuals of vision, with the ability to convert their ideas into successful institutions and enterprises. One of the earliest of these was naturalist, writer, philosopher, and wilderness advocate Sigurd Olson, who moved to Ely to teach in 1923. Olson was Joe Seliga's biology teacher during Seliga's freshman year. Years later, the author hired Joe to restore his prized E. M. White and B. N. Morris wood-and-canvas canoes Olson later gained fame for his uncompromising stands on the value of wilderness, and shared his experiences and thoughts in a number of popular books.

Among more recent transplants who have contributed to Ely's preeminence as a center of freethinking achievers are polar explorers Paul Schurke and Will Steger. The men were partners on a grueling 57-day dogsled trek to the North Pole in 1986, the first team to accomplish the elusive goal without support equipment and food drops. Since then, each has led other remarkable expeditions and focused attention on the causes of cross-cultural fellowship and the planet's fragile ecosystems.

Steger still recalls the rainy October day in 1970, shortly after he arrived in Ely, when he walked into town from his then-roadless property. He had heard good things about a local canoe builder and wanted to meet him. He hoped he wouldn't be turned away at the door, wet and unkempt as he was. Of course, he needn't have worried.

"Joe didn't mind my abrupt intrusion or the many questions that I had for him" Steger recalls. "Meeting the craftsman in his setting, surrounded by hanging tools and jigs, in his shop permeated by the

Many local mushers offer dogsled adventures in the region around Ely, allowing clients to experience the thrill of winter camping.

The upper Midwest is a hotbed of cross-country skiing, and the Ely area is no exception.

The displays and programs featured at the International Wolf Center help cast the role of the timberwolf as a natural predator in a realistic light. The captive wolves at the center, however, are always the main attraction.

sweet smell of cedar was a moment I will never forget. Later as I dried out in his warm kitchen and his wife, Nora, poured me tea I felt impressed, not only with the man's skill, but with the man himself. He was kind, humble and willing to share. He was a true gentleman who had character I found worth emulating."

Steger's former wife, Patti Holmberg, and Schurke's wife, Susan, have turned their experience outfitting the demanding expeditions with mukluks and anoraks in the Inuit tradition into thriving retail businesses. Patti's Steger Mukluks and Susan's Wintergreen Designs each have prominent retail spaces in town, extensive catalog sales, and international recognition; together, they provide nearly 100 local jobs.

Bob Cary mentions several other relative newcomers who have made names for themselves, among them Jim Brandenburg, who moved to Ely in 1981, and Steve and Nancy Piragis, who arrived in the region from back East in the 1970s as graduate students on state and EPA research projects. When they married, they decided to make Ely their home. Beginning with a tiny enterprise selling high-quality woodstoves from an old service station, Steve gradually shifted to canoes, canoe accessories, and outfitting. Today, Piragis Northwoods Outfitters' retail store sits on a prominent corner on Sheridan, joined at the hip with the Chocolate Moose, a highly rated restaurant built of logs, which the couple also started but no longer own. Beneath canoes and kayaks of all descriptions hanging from the retail space ceiling, shoppers find a colorful variety of paddling gear, outdoor clothing, and northwoods crafts and gifts. Upstairs is an independently run bookstore with an emphasis on natural history and the northwoods. Steve and Nancy's Boundary Waters Catalog is a major arm of the business that provides another 50 local jobs. The outfitting enterprise is unusual for its canoe and kayak trips to exotic destinations like Patagonia, Zimbabwe, Thailand, the Aleutian Islands, and Vietnam. Piragis International Expeditions is a reflection of the experience, research, and confidence the couple has accumulated over 20 years. Despite the widespread recognition, Steve and Nancy remain strong members of the Ely community.

Steve owns a Seliga canoe, a rare model with a "Y" stern—a small transom capable of handling an outboard, but still good for paddling. For years he has provided Joe with the close-celled foam he uses to make yoke pads for his canoes.

"Steve's helped me out quite a bit getting the special foam," Joe offers. "If he didn't have it at the store, he'd drop what he was doing and run out (to the warehouse) to get some. If he was out of stock and I needed some, he'd order it and have it for me in a couple of days. Steve's a regular guy that way."

Will Steger

Paul Schurke, left, and Will Steger at the North Pole in 1986.
Both Artic explorers live in the Ely area.

The odds of a town Ely's size having two internationally celebrated polar explorers would seem long, but that is exactly the case.

Like his neighbor, Paul Schurke, Will Steger hit the ground running immediately after the pair's 1986 odyssey and has never stopped. Steger's second book, *Saving the Earth,* co-authored with Jon Bowermaster, reveals the direction in which his interests now lie. The peril in which we now find the Earth because of environmental degradation has been the subject of numerous Steger lectures and appearances, and the underlying impetus behind his most recent expeditions.

By the time Steger discovered Ely at age 19, he was already a seasoned traveler of the Canadian Arctic. Adventure—especially of the northern variety—hooked the Minneapolis-born Steger at an early age. He was returning home from a lengthy canoe trip in Canada when he happened to end up in the Ely area. Intrigued, he spent some time looking around and found a piece of land outside town that suited him perfectly. He purchased it, planning to return and settle there after college.

Steger moved to Ely and began building a home that came to be known as the Homestead, a perfect base for sled dogs and staging and training for expeditions. Over the next 10 years, Steger continued honing his skills while traveling throughout Canada and Alaska. The trips became increasingly longer and challenging, and in 1985 he completed a solo 5,000-mile dogsled journey from his home to Point Barrow, Alaska. The following year, Steger, Schurke, and six teammates reached the North Pole after 56 days of travel.

With the planet's environment becoming an increasing priority for Steger, it was inevitable that he would turn his focus to Antarctica, one of the earth's most fragile ecosystems. To build awareness of Antarctica's unique ecology, Steger decided an "ordinary" dogsled trip to the South Pole would not do. He proposed crossing the entire continent—3,700 miles—and began organizing a trip of mammoth proportions. To be certain the expedition received worldwide attention, he assembled the International Trans-Antarctica Team consisting of six men from different nations and 36 specially bred dogs. The team's successful 220-day crossing of the continent was nothing short of epic. Steger and Bowermaster retold the compelling tale in their book *Crossing Antarctica.*

Today, Will Steger remains constantly engaged, conceiving new ways to relate his urgent message to people everywhere. The Homestead outside Ely is often the site of intense planning on a global scale—planning rooted in the belief that appreciation for the earth is best realized through self-powered and arduous trips in existing wilderness areas.

Paul Schurke

For some Ely residents, the weather is just not cold enough; at least that seems to be the case with Paul Schurke. For years now, the Minneapolis native has been forsaking northern Minnesota, often in the dead of winter, for the far north—sometimes as far north as you can possibly get: the Pole itself.

Schurke moved to Ely in 1977 and was already spending extended periods of time traveling through northern Canada and Alaska. Between 1977 and 1983, he started a program called "Wilderness Inquiry" that specialized in providing wilderness access for the disabled.

By 1986, he had enough experience under his belt to co-lead a daring assault on the North Pole by a talented group of dog mushers. His partner on the expedition was his Ely neighbor and fellow northern traveler, Will Steger. Their expedition was distinguished from others by the fact that they used no resupply support, but rather carried everything they required. The arduous adventure was fraught with nearly impassable ice formations, perilous sea openings, blizzards, and unbelievable discomfort in chill factors well below -100 degrees Fahrenheit. The mission's success ensured Schurke and Steger places in the annals of polar exploration. The pair wrote vividly of the experience in their best-selling book *North to the Pole*.

However, that was only the beginning for Paul Schurke. After much thought and research, he decided to concentrate his energy on a new venture he called the Bering Bridge Project. The goal of the project was to reunite or at least re-establish contact between the Inuit of Siberia and those of Alaska, historically a thin bond that had been severed by the Cold War. Bering Bridge culminated with a joint dogsled expedition by members of both cultures traveling through eastern Siberia, crossing the icebound Bering Sea and penetrating western Alaska for some distance.

Schurke's most recent projects have focused on the training of Chinese scientists from The Academy of Sciences for survival, travel, and scientific work in the world's Polar regions. Another of Schurke's interests is the Inuit culture along Greenland's northwest coast. He has visited the region several times and is friends and has traveled with some of the inhabitants, including descendents of the North Pole's discoverers, Robert Peary and Matthew Henson.

Closer to home, where Paul spends much of his time, he is kept busy running Wintergreen Lodge, which organizes dogsled trips between lodges and cabins, and offers programs in environmental education and winter travel in the back country. Paul's wife, Susan, is the founder and owner of Wintergreen Designs in Ely, which produces beautifully functional anoraks, parkas, hats, and mittens, and employs 40 local residents.

Replacing the well-paying jobs lost when the mines closed has not been easy, and there has been no blueprint to follow. These profiles represent only a few of the responses the resourceful people of Ely, both native and transplanted, have developed. At the industrial park on Miner's Drive alongside Steger Mukluks is a branch of a national travel agency that arranges trips for organizations nationwide. There's also an arm of the Minnesota State Revenue Service, perhaps the town's largest employer these days. It can be argued that most of these jobs are not as high-paying as those once offered by the mines, but it can likewise be pointed out that for the most part they are less hazardous and more friendly to the environment. And if any one of these employers is forced to shut its doors, it will not directly affect hundreds of households all at once.

Ely was born tough and resourceful and these traits have allowed the town to survive and to redefine itself in a new and vital way. The old days are memories here like everywhere else, and the choices the people of Ely have made have helped make it more interesting than many other localities that have faced similar disruption.

Just outside Ely on the road to Winton is the International Wolf Center, an impressive complex shared with the Kawishiwi Wilderness Station, where adventurers can obtain Boundary Waters entry permits. The Wolf Center's fascinating displays depict the wolf's role in nature and challenge our perceptions of the wolf throughout history. Only recently have programs like the one at the center made the average person aware of the fact that the wolf is merely another fellow creature, trying by his wits to make his way as best he can. Captive wolves in the natural enclosure behind the center, visible through the large plate-glass windows, have given thousands of people a close-up of this enigmatic creature, which turns out to be not as evil and threatening as it is misunderstood.

Ely, Minnesota, had a wolf at its door when the mines closed down in the 1960s. But for many it turned out to be not as dark and threatening as first perceived. Once options were identified, the town forged ahead, largely with the wise use of the region's natural beauty. Today, instead of a wolf at the door, this impressive wild creature is a living symbol of the wilderness so many have come to associate with the town—and are so willing to come experience.

Coming of Age at the Edge of the Wilderness

Joe's grandparents, Ann and Michel Seliga, are shown outside their cabin near Shagawa Lake in 1911 with Stephen and Anna. Stephen, Jr., is in suspenders before his father, while Anna holds the infant Joe. Joe's sister Ann is at right in front of the potted plants. *Joe Seliga Collection*

Twenty-three-year-old Joe Seliga was up against it. It was early May 1934, and he and his father Stephen had put their canoe on the Nina Moose River where it flowed beneath the Echo Trail, hoping to spice up the family's larder with some lake trout from Big Moose Lake. When the father and son saw how high the water was from the spring rains and snow runoff, they figured they might be rushing the season. But there was no harm in trying. Or so they thought.

Now, as Joe fought his way through the brush along the streamside portage, he knew his father had encountered trouble while paddling the lightened canoe through the swollen rapids. Joe's heart sank when he saw the overturned B. N. Morris, pinned by a fallen tree and beating up and down in the turbulent water. For an instant, he feared the worst but, thankfully, there was his father, pulling himself out of the current by clutching at the streamside alders. Stephen Seliga was soaked, near freezing, and on the wrong side of the river, but he was tough and he was okay.

A gathering of paddlers in 1907. Stephen's two B. N. Morris canoes are against a dock at Shagawa Lake, the 18-footer on the left, the 15-footer on the right. Stephen is in the stern of the 15-footer at far right, and Anna holds their daughter, Ann. Notice the sleeves Stephen is wearing to protect his white shirt. *Joe Seliga Collection*

Now Joe had to figure out a way to retrieve the broken canoe from the current's grip, reach his shivering father, get them back to the car parked a few miles upstream, and beat a retreat back to their warm home in Ely.

Such were the risks associated with a life that was intensely connected to the northern Minnesota border country in the early twentieth century and depended partially on the bounty of the northwoods for variety and a margin of security. In fact, those northwoods and the town of Ely nestled there remain such an integral part of Joe Seliga that there is really no way to consider his life and work without putting them in the context of the town and its surrounding region. Likewise, the incident on the Nina Moose would prove an equally formative influence on the life of young Joe Seliga, sending him on an adventure that has thus far spanned more than six decades and earned respect and admiration wherever fine canoes and the outdoors are appreciated.

The Challenges of a New Land

Joe's paternal grandparents arrived in Ely in 1890, with the town's first wave of immigrants. It was the same year that Ely was incorporated and just two years after a railroad line first connected the

Sigurd Olson

"This is the most beautiful lake country on the continent. We can afford to cherish and protect it. Some places should be preserved from development or exploitation, for they satisfy human need for solace, belonging, and perspective. In the end, we turn to nature in a frenzied chaotic world, there to find silence—oneness-wholeness-spiritual release"

— Quoted by Becky Rom
Undated pamphlet produced by the Friends of the Boundary Waters Wilderness

Sigurd Olson—author, wilderness advocate, philosopher, and Ely resident from 1932 until his death in 1982—relaxes inside his beloved cabin on Listening Point at Burntside Lake. *Photo by Don Albright. Courtesy of R. K. Olson, Listening Point Foundation*

So spoke Sigurd Olson, testifying at a congressional field hearing in Ely in 1977, regarding the Fraser Bill that sought to enact full wilderness protection for the Boundary Waters Canoe Area (BWCA). Tall, leather-skinned, with a full head of white hair, Olson stood patiently at the microphone as hundreds of fellow townspeople, many of whom had been his neighbors for half a century, attempted to distract and prevent him from speaking with a chorus of jeers, yells, and catcalls. Outside in the parking lot, other opponents were hanging the "radical" in effigy.

Olson, then 78 years old, ignored the disruption and spoke calmly and clearly of his support for, and the wisdom behind, full protection for the lake-bejeweled swatch of wilderness that was so close to his heart. Eventually, despite the local opposition, Olson's views prevailed the following year when President Jimmy Carter signed into law expanded wilderness protection, launching the Boundary Waters Canoe Area Wilderness (BWCAW).

Not long after the hearing, Olson received a visitor at the writing shack he kept near his home— his former high-school biology student, Joe Seliga. Joe had come to tell the famous writer and conservationist that, although he didn't agree with every point in his testimony, he had a great respect for Olson's courage in facing the hostile gathering and unflinchingly speaking his piece. He asked "Sig" if he'd ever regretted getting involved in the process. After a pause, Olson answered, "Well, Joe, you and I have seen the best of it."

Olson could only have been referring to the border country itself, which was vast and still nearly inaccessible except by canoe when he first arrived in the region (and Seliga was still a youngster) 50 years earlier.

Sigurd Olson was born in Chicago in 1899 and was educated at the University of Wisconsin in Madison in agriculture and geology. He married Elizabeth Uhrenholdt in 1921, and the couple spent their honeymoon canoeing the lake country outside Ely. Two years later he accepted a position teaching science at Ely's Memorial High School and worked summers as a canoe guide, eventually starting an outfitting business. In 1932 he earned a master's degree in zoology, with a thesis based on his studies of the timberwolf, and returned to Ely as a full-time teacher at Ely Junior College, becoming the dean in 1936.

When the Wilderness Society was launched in 1935, Olson became a charter member and spent the rest of his life tirelessly promoting and lobbying for wilderness causes. In 1953 he became president of the National Parks Association, and a few years later was elected to the governing council of the Wilderness Society.

Sigurd Olson had published numerous articles in outdoor magazines before his first book, *The Singing Wilderness*, was published in 1956. His second book, *Listening Point*, got its title from Olson's cherished log cabin on Burntside Lake. Olson's writing is often philosophical yet passionate, earning him an international following interested not only in outdoor adventure, but also in the importance of wildness to human well-being in a modern age. Olson published six more books after Listening Point, receiving the John Burroughs Medal for Wilderness Days. He died of a heart attack in January 1982 while snowshoeing outside his Ely home.

The Listening Point Foundation is headquartered in Hayward, Wisconsin, and maintains Sigurd Olson's legacy of wilderness education and preservation, as well as his cabin on Burntside Lake. Olson's son, Robert, presides over the Foundation's Board of Directors.

These pictures were taken on May 14, 1911, little more than a month after Joe Seliga was born. Above: Joe's father Stephen stands at the stern of the 18-foot Morris. The man on the right is family friend Bob Nuff, and the boy with the pike is Nuff's son. Below: Stephen Seliga, Sr., at the bow of his prized Morris canoe. *Joe Seliga Collection*

B. N. Morris Canoes

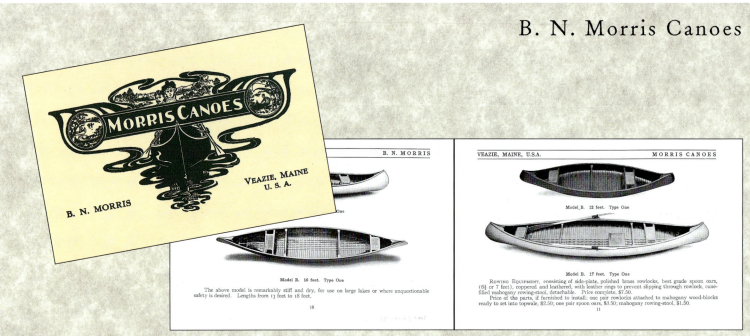

Pictured at lower right in this spread from the 1908 B. N. Morris catalog is a 17-foot Model B with oarlocks, likely identical to those on Stephen Seliga's 18-foot Morris. *Courtesy Wooden Canoe Heritage Association, Ltd.*

Maine's Penobscot River, especially the stretch between Old Town and tidewater at Bangor, is recognized as the cradle of wooden canoe manufacturing. E. H. Gerrish launched the wood-and-canvas canoe industry from his Bangor shop in the late-1870s. In the Old Town area, both E. M. White and Guy Carlton had head starts on an eventual giant, Old Town Canoe, which would quickly dominate the business. However, in the eyes of many aficionados, the finest of all the early wood-and-canvas canoes were manufactured in the little town of Veazie, exactly midway between the two better known cities, by the B. N. Morris Canoe Company.

The graceful appearance, shapely lines, and impeccable workmanship were what made a Morris canoe special. Most were built for use as pleasure craft, as opposed to the more utilitarian design built primarily for guides, fisherman, and foresters. The leisure canoe clubs that flourished in the East placed a premium on craft that featured sweeping sheerlines, high ends, and narrow entries, yet were wide and stable enough to keep from shipping water or flipping if an amorous couple aboard got to shifting around as darkness fell. Fancy paint jobs, often with gold-leaf filigree, were also popular.

The exact date the B. N. Morris Canoe Company started appears to have gotten earlier each time the company put out a new brochure, but it's not impossible that it was launched as early as 1887, when founder Bert Morris was just 21 years old. Morris' talent and business acumen were well developed for such a young man, and by 1910 he had 35 employees in a large, wood-framed factory that had already been enlarged twice. By 1920—about 13 or 14 years after Stephen Seliga, Sr., purchased the family's cherished 18-foot Morris—75 employees worked at the plant; that same year, a tragic fire leveled most of the uninsured facility, bringing large-scale production of the popular canoes to a premature halt. Arson was suspected but never proven.

Since Bert Morris could either not afford or was unwilling to rebuild (or both), most of his experienced craftsmen found jobs with other area canoe factories. His foreman, Walter Grant, went to work for the Kennebec Canoe Company in Waterville, Maine, and Old Town Canoe bought much of the material that escaped the flames. Bert did some work for Old Town and also set up a one-man shop near his Veazie home, where he continued to build a limited number of designs to special order. In 1938, Joe wrote to Bert Morris inquiring about the prospects of becoming a Morris dealer. "Bert Morris wrote back saying his canoe building was just a hobby in those days," recalls Joe. "He didn't want to get into anything where he'd have to produce canoes to fill orders. But it was a real nice letter."

Morris died in 1940 at age 74, having made a big splash in the canoe industry at a very young age. After the fire, however, he lived out his life in a respectable and quiet manner. Many of his company's lovely canoes have survived to this day, and are eagerly sought by collectors, and builder Rollin Thurlow of Atkinson, Maine, produces some replicas.

This Seliga family portrait was taken around 1926. Stephen and Anna are seated in front; Joe is second from the left in back. *Joe Seliga Collection*

mining outpost with the rest of the world. Accompanying the Seligas was their young son Stephen, who would grow up, work, and raise a large family in Ely. Just as importantly, Stephen would quickly grasp the essence of the northern wilderness. Fishing, hunting, berrying, and picnicking would become year-round institutions in the Seliga household—and inseparable from these activities were canoes and the ability to use them well. Stephen Seliga's interest in and skill with canoes would play a major role in the life of his second son and ensure widespread respect for the Seliga name.

Michel Seliga and his wife Ann haled from the area of the Austro-Hungarian Empire that would become Czechoslovakia after World War I. Stephen was just seven years old when the family immigrated to the United States, where opportunities were said to await anyone willing to work hard, risk an ocean voyage in steerage, and face the challenges of a new land and language. Somehow, Michel got word of mining jobs in the rugged north country, and was either bold or desperate enough to take the chance. The risk paid off, and Michel and Ann eventually settled into a cabin near Shagawa Lake, in what must have been a robust and rustic community.

Early Ely seems to have suited young Stephen just fine, but like any young man, he found the possibility of a high-paying job in a different part of the country irresistible. Just such a temptation lured him to Pittsburgh, where he worked as an oiler for a short time as a teenager. It didn't take him long, however, to appreciate the life he had left behind and to realize that slightly better money in a busy and, in those days, dingy city was no substitute for decent work in a true paradise. Soon, he was back home.

At age 18, Stephen was hired on at Gleason's Hardware Store, located at the site now occupied by Cranberry's Restaurant and Saloon in Ely. The work suited him, but the pay was less than that in the mines, even the temporary labor positions above ground, one of which he took at the Chandler operation after two years at Gleason's. It was a fortunate move in at least one respect. When a fellow worker showed Stephen a photograph of a young female cousin back in the home country, the young Seliga was immediately infatuated. He wrote her a letter and her response initiated a furious round of correspondence that ended when Stephen sent Anna fare for passage to America, including a train ticket to Ely. The pair were taken with each other as much in person as they had been through photographs and letters. There was a brief courtship and a wedding—Stephen was 23 and Anna was 18.

With a wife and to support and a child on the way, Stephen took on extra work, for a time as an assistant to the town undertaker and as a part-time custodian at the school. In 1909, he landed a full-time position as a painter for the U.S. Steel Corporation. In addition to mine structures that needed painting and maintenance, company-owned worker housing also had to be kept up.

Joseph T. Seliga came along on April 11, 1911, the fourth of 12 children. He was preceded by Ann, who was born within a year of their parents' wedding; Stephen, Jr., who was born two years later; and Rose, who died in infancy. John followed on Joe's heels a year later, and was in turn followed by Margaret, Helen, Dorothy, Rudolph, and Albert, who died at age six. Brother Daniel, 15 years Joe's junior, was killed in the Battle of the Bulge at just 18 years of age. The youngest Seliga sibling, Ethel, was born two years after Daniel.

The used 1924 Model T Ford that Joe's father purchased in 1927 gave the family new mobility, previously undreamed of. *Joe Seliga Collection*

"There were lots of big families in those days," Joe recalls. "But, still, ours was one of the biggest. There was always something to do," he adds, grinning, "and you could usually get somebody to help you, too."

A Good Measure of Fun

It was an impressive brood, requiring Anna's full attention, a good income provided by Stephen, Sr., and a roomy home, which the couple built on White Street in 1915 when Joe was four years old. The area behind the house in those days was mostly woods and fields, an ideal playground, with trees and logs to climb, paths on which to run, shaded grottos beside brooks, and frog ponds waiting to be explored. Playing in the woods just outside town remains one of Joe's fondest memories of growing up in a close family and sharing a good measure of fun along with the work and responsibilities. "It's all built up now," Joe says of the area, which includes the lot on which his current house now sits. "When I was a kid, everything beyond the house was just fields and woods. I was running around out there whenever I had a chance—every time I could escape."

Like their neighbors, the Seligas kept a large garden and the children were expected to do their part in its preparation, maintenance, and harvest. In addition, there were wild berries to pick, especially the sweet blueberries that grew close to the ground among boulders in the clearings that began to surround town as the dense forests were opened up. In July 1911, three-month-old Joe was bundled up, set in the family canoe, and taken along as his parents made their annual day trip along lakeshores, where the berries were juicy and accessible. A few years later, it was not uncommon for Joe and a random group of siblings to be driven into the countryside in the morning and dropped off near a berry thicket with a bushel basket in hand. Later that afternoon, Stephen and Anna would return for them, expecting the basket to be full. Safety was never a concern in those days; other than infrequent shady political dealings, bar fights, and occasional poaching, there was little crime around town, and the region's black bears were generally shy and elusive.

Of course, school intruded upon the lives of children in early-twentieth century Ely, just as it does today. Joe showed up for kindergarten in 1916 at the Washington School, which was built just the year before, right across the way from the Seligas' White Street house. He was almost immediately advanced to the first grade, making him one of the youngest members of his class. With little thought or fuss, Joe breezed through the grades with his school chums.

One of the few regrets that Joe has from his youth is the fact that he and his siblings were seldom encouraged to learn the language from the "old country." In fact, in most cases, children were forbidden to speak in their parents' or grandparents' tongue because it was considered an impediment to success in American society. "My father was such a patriot," Joe remarks, "that he said to us, 'We're Americans now, and in this house we're going to speak American.'" Although Stephen and Anna might occasionally converse with their parents and other adult immigrants, the children were not invited to learn or participate. Cooking, however, was another matter—the flavorful dishes of the old country appeared frequently on the tables of Ely's immigrant families and were generally relished.

In 1924, Joe was among the members of the first freshman class to enter Ely's brand-new, three-story Memorial High School. His academic interests were history and chemistry, with math, especially geometry, being his least favorite. Sigurd Olson, who had moved to town a couple of years earlier, was Joe's biology teacher and a good one, as Joe remembers, though he has few comments on Olson's teaching abilities. Not being especially tall or large, Seliga did not participate in athletics in high school. Besides, he favored outdoor activities like hunting and fishing over football practice, and in 1928, he graduated from Memorial High along with 90 classmates.

Small-Town Living

While Joe was growing up, Ely was transforming itself from a frontier outpost into the typical American small town and was taking great joy in the same recreational activities and celebrations as similar towns across the country. One popular summer activity Joe recalls was baseball. Pickup games were common at the city's municipal ball field, schoolyards, and any other place where there was a flat piece of ground and a few youngsters with gloves and a bat. The town team was stocked with young working men—not a few of them employed in various municipal departments—and a few of the better high school ball players. With the growing number of decent roads connecting the region's towns, the Ely nine played a schedule that included teams from several surrounding communities, and Joe remembers attending some of the bigger games as a child.

The Fourth of July was the signature summer event and was excitedly anticipated by nearly everyone. Kids were paid a quarter to march alongside bands, civic organizations, and veterans in the parade that usually proceeded up Chapman Street to Whiteside Park. At the parade's end, an official read the Declaration of Independence in its entirety, which was followed by a picnic from baskets that were packed at home and supplemented by concessions. As soon as everyone's cold fried chicken and pie had settled, or even if it hadn't, the town was treated to a baseball game, generally between the town team and the archrival Winton nine. As evening wore on and more beer was consumed, impromptu wrestling matches might keep the crowd entertained until a climactic fireworks display capped the festivities.

Seliga remembers other events that punctuated the daily routine of life in Ely, among them automobile exhibitions in the days before auto dealerships and logging expositions featuring contests like crosscut-sawing, speed-chopping, and axe-throwing. One spectacle that particularly stands out in his memory is a visit to Ely by a traveling Winchester sharpshooter named Al Topperwin. Among the feats performed by this straight-shooting professional were "drawing" images on cardboard with rounds from a .22-caliber rifle and keeping a washtub spinning in the air with repeated shotgun blasts. "He was some good shot," Joe says, the glint in his eye flashing. "And, you know, it was right in town behind some buildings in a little field. I don't know how come no one was hit. They'd never let you do that nowadays."

The legendary cold of the northern Minnesota winter was not deep enough to completely congeal social life in the community. Folks got around on the snowy streets, making social calls, patronizing ethnic clubs and bars, and supporting the high school basketball team. If good ice formed early and the snow held off, there were large skating parties with great bonfires on Shagawa

Lake, as well as at the expansive municipal rink at the present location of Whiteside Park.

For Joe Seliga, the best times centered on the outdoors: family picnics at nearby lakes, fishing, and canoeing. His earliest memory is of crawling around in the bottom of a canoe, inside the enveloping curves of its ribs, listening to the soft murmur of the water against the canvas-covered planking. In 1905, his father Stephen had taken advantage of an opportunity to buy a barely used 15-foot canoe from a young mining engineer who was being transferred to a new location. The wood-and-canvas canoe had been manufactured in Veazie, Maine, by B. N. Morris Boat & Canoe Company, which was incorporated around 1884 and was an early player in the commercial canoe industry. A year or two later, the elder Seliga bought another Morris, a new 18-foot Model D with a fine pair of oars for rowing from a special seat near the canoe's center. The canoe's serial number, 4101, indicated it was built at the Maine factory in 1904 and was the one hundred-first canoe built that year. The styling and the impeccable workmanship of the Morris canoes would make a deep impression on Joe and haunt him until years later, when he would figure out how to build one just as elegant.

At the time, boating and canoeing were becoming popular recreational activities around Ely, as in similar regions throughout the country; a locally built steamer carried passengers around nearby Shagawa Lake. There were liveries where families who didn't own a canoe could rent one, and the surface of neighboring lakes were commonly peppered with small craft throughout the summer. Many weekend boaters paddled or rowed their craft up Burntside River to the lake, where they took advantage of a planked portage trail near the site of Burntside Lodge, which has been in business since 1913. Water flowing swiftly down a long sluiceway at Burntside Dam presented a great temptation to intrepid paddlers, and Joe remembers a photo showing a string of fine Morris canoes, the paddlers grinning as they sped down the big water slide toward the surface of the river below. Seliga claims he never tried such a stunt himself. "It looked dangerous to me," he laughs, "but those guys looked like they were having a hell of a time. 'Course, you don't know what happened to them when they hit (the lake's surface)."

Adventures in the Beloved B. N. Morris

Stephen Seliga kept his canoes in a small Shagawa Lake boathouse that was leased from his employer, U.S. Steel, not an uncommon benefit of the day. Since automobiles were scarce and roof racks unknown, the accommodations allowed the family easy access to the lakes whenever they embarked on an outing—and between family picnics and fishing excursions this was fairly often.

Fishing trips often ranged beyond Burntside, with Stephen taking the boys the length of the sprawling lake and then portaging into Slim, Fenske, or Bass Lake. Their skill with canoes also enabled the Seligas to expand their hunting range to waterfowling spots like Rice Lake and fine "partridge" cover in roadless areas well outside of town. Joe recalls one grouse-hunting trip that was cut short by a sudden, very intense snowstorm. Deep in the woods, he was turned around by the changing aspect of the terrain as wind-driven snow swirled around him, causing near-whiteout conditions. Luckily, Joe was still within earshot of his father's signal shots, which provided him with some direction. The pair started for home with the 18-foot Morris half full of snow and the white stuff still coming down hard. Like most outdoorsmen of the era, the Seligas packed a heavy canvas tent for their shelter afield. Anna prepared hearty fare for the men to take with them, which they supplemented with fish and game, as it became available.

When Joe was 16, the 18-foot Morris was stolen from the boathouse and went missing for nearly a year before a tip led the Seligas to a boathouse on White Iron Lake. Although the perpetrator had covered the beautifully varnished interior of the canoe with house paints in an attempt to disguise it, the stamped serial numbers were still legible on the stems. The owner of the boathouse, who may well not have been the original thief, claimed he had bought the canoe and was not willing to give it up. Joe's father thought enough of the Morris, however, to hire a lawyer, and for the then considerable sum of $21 in legal fees, the canoe was returned to the Seligas and no charges filed. Though they were grateful to have the canoe back, the Seligas were dismayed by the ugly painted interior. Joe decided to do something about it. Stripping and refinishing the Morris' interior would be the first large-scale canoe work of his career, and by the time he was finished, the canoe was as beautiful as the day his father had bought it.

In 1926, a new "highway" opened in the area, looping around the eastern end of Shagawa Lake before heading off to the north, skirting the east and north arms of Burntside Lake, and continuing on to Big Lake and eventually to Crane Lake. To the sportsmen lucky enough to own an automobile, the Echo Trail opened a world of new opportunities, places that were once the exclusive province of those willing and able to paddle and portage a canoe. Never one to be left behind, Joe's father purchased a 1924 Model T Ford the following year, providing his family with new mobility previously unimagined. Family outings and berrying excursions extended to new locations even farther afield, as did the men's hunting and fishing trips. Commercial roof racks were unknown in those days, but the large projecting fenders of the Model T made a suitable support on which to lash and carry a canoe. On any weekend, Stephen Seliga and his sons could now reach hotspots that they might otherwise have gotten to only once a year.

Naturally there was more to life than picnics and fishing trips. Pocket money was something that had to be earned, and the sooner one started, the better. Although it was difficult for any high schooler in the 1920s to obtain a steady job, Joe managed to land employment while he was still a junior in high school. It was just a couple years after Louis Pasteur had developed the process for disinfecting milk that bears his name, and testing cows for tuberculosis was still a part of every veterinarian's repertoire. Joe assisted the local vet with this task, visiting the small farms and back-lot dairy cows that furnished Ely with its fresh milk, taking blood samples for analysis. Likewise, the chlorinization of municipal water supplies was not yet a universal practice, and young Seliga found another part-time job with the town's water board. The purification process in those days consisted of adding alum and soda ash to the water before it passed through sand and gravel filters to an underground storage tank, from which it was pumped into the municipal water tank. Joe's job involved shoveling the alum and ash from barrels into the water, as well as drawing water samples for testing.

"I Was a Goner"

In 1928, Joe graduated from Memorial High School, an inauspicious time to enter the work force in isolated Ely, Minnesota, or anyplace else. In just over a year, the October 1929 stock-market crash would mark the official start of the Great Depression and the hard times that Joe, a lifelong Democrat, refers to as the "Hoover Days." Still, he landed his first mine-related job with U. S. Steel in 1930. It proved to be difficult work, lugging, on his shoulders, 10-foot-long timbers called "caps" from the termini of underground tracks to whatever radiating tunnels were in the process of being shored up. In addition to the timbers, stringy, axe-split jackpine boards called "lagging" that were used to keep the tunnel ceilings from dropping down had to be carried by hand to work sites from the ends of the rail spurs. However, being fit and young, and with no other options, Joe was not overly critical of the exhausting work.

As the Depression tightened its grip on the nation, steady jobs everywhere dried up and workers landed out on the street. When Joe's mine job ended just over a year later, part-time work

Eleanor "Nora" Krogar sent Joe this photo before they started dating in 1931. Nora's inscription on the back reads, "The snow sure was bright, honey, but not bad, is it?" As Joe recalls, "After I saw it, I was a goner." *Joe Seliga Collection*

Joe and Nora shortly after they were married in 1932.
Joe Seliga Collection

was about all that was available in Ely, and Joe picked up odd painting, carpentry, and groundskeeping jobs. A single man living at home with his parents, watching his pennies, catching plenty of fish, and shooting enough game could always get by.

But fate doesn't always make things so simple. In 1931, at 20 years old, Joe met Eleanor Krogar of Biwabik, Minnesota. He was lovestruck. When she sent him a picture of herself standing before an iron fence, Joe realized she was the prettiest girl he'd ever known. "When I got that picture," Joe smiles, "I was a goner."

To complicate matters, Eleanor was only visiting her sister in Ely and actually resided 50 long miles away, a considerable distance in a time of two-lane gravel roads. The attraction was mutual, however, and the couple began affording themselves every opportunity to see one another. Joe hitched rides to Biwabik on weekends and "Nora" spent as much time as possible at her sister's place. Before long, Joe and Eleanor were engaged and set a wedding date for late March of the following year.

It wouldn't be easy. Both were living with their parents, 50 miles apart, and Seliga's employment picture was still very sketchy. Few municipal work projects were being funded, yet Joe got work cutting dead trees, thinning and burning brush, and shoveling gravel for $3.41 a day and a maximum of 60 hours a week at the new airport that was under construction.

It wasn't much, and the couple could not hope to own or even rent a home of their own at first, but they loved each other desperately and knew they belonged together. So, on March 29, 1932, before a justice of the peace, Joseph T. Seliga took Eleanor Krogar as his wife, beginning a loving partnership that would hold firm through the Depression, World War II, and every other challenge the next 68 years could hold.

At first, the couple lived apart during the week, with Joe working in Ely and joining his bride at her folks' house on weekends—far from ideal, but certainly better than nothing. In January 1933, President Franklin Roosevelt took office and rapidly implemented civil work projects like the Civil Works Administration (CWA), Works Progress Administration (WPA), and Civilian Conservation Corps (CCC). That same year, adding to the young couple's financial responsibilities, was the birth in Biwabik of their first child, Richard. It became more important than ever for the couple to be together on more than just weekends, so an apartment was fixed up on the second floor of Stephen and Anna's residence on White Street, and it became another temporary home for Joe, Nora, and Richard.

With Joe permanently back in town, it was natural to get back into the routine of hunting and fishing with his brothers and especially his father. With money tight and many mouths to feed, the walleyes, lake trout, grouse, and deer were welcome additions to the family larder.

Incident on the Nina Moose
Twenty-five miles or so northwest of Ely, the Nina Moose River crosses under the Echo Trail, connecting a small chain of lakes teeming with walleyes and lake trout. The best time to catch these fish was in the early spring, and although the water level was extremely high, in May 1934, Joe and his father loaded the 18-foot Morris onto the car's fender wells and set off on a weekend expedition to make the first big catch of the season. The water was even higher and cooler than they expected, depressing the fishing and making canoe travel a tricky proposition. Between Big Moose and Nina Moose lakes, a portage trail offered an alternative to a rough stretch of rapids. When the Seligas reached the trail, they found it flooded, with a large volume of water tumbling over the rocks out in the river. It would be too risky to run in a loaded canoe, but Stephen foresaw little difficulty in taking the canoe down empty while his son portaged the gear down the wet trail. They'd used similar strategy many times before.

Joe's troubles on the soupy portage trail, crisscrossed with winter's fallen trees, took all his attention, but he stopped short when he heard an unfamiliar and very disturbing sound above the loud rush of the freshet. As Joe recalls, "I was carrying the big pack along the portage trail when I heard a strange sound, even over the water. It was terrible. It was like someone taking a stick and breaking it over his knee, only maybe a dozen sticks. I dropped my pack and ran through the brush to the shore."

Joe scrambled to the bank just in time to see his soaking wet father struggling to pull himself onto the far shore. His relief was only momentary, however—a glance out on the channel filled the young man with a hopeless dread. Out in the fast water, still pinned by the beaver-felled tree that had snagged it, was the beloved Morris, capsized and broken, beating up and down in the current.

The father and son team had to think fast. They were still a long way from the road, and abandoning the cherished canoe was unthinkable. Joe managed to throw a rock attached to a fishing line across to Stephen, by which means the father pulled a rope over to his side. Using this line for a measure of safety, he was able to make a frigid crossing to his son, attaching a line to the trapped canoe at the same time. Using their combined strength, they pulled the canoe free of the snag and hauled it ashore. An initial inspection of the damage was truly discouraging: the sides and bottom of the canoe were badly out of shape and the whole craft flexed oddly—21 frames, called ribs, were cracked or broken, many of them badly. Luckily, the canvas covering was still intact, and if they could figure out a way to reinforce the broken wood, they might still paddle out.

There were plenty of alder saplings along the bank, as well as the hulk of a burned-out tree, and the pair still had their axe. They discovered they could force the ribs roughly back into shape around the hollowed tree and hold them in place with saplings and copper wire they had brought along to use as weight for their fishing line. When they were done, the canoe had regained some of its original stiffness. Also, to their great surprise, it barely leaked when they put it in the quiet water below the rapids. They carefully loaded up, got in, and paddled the several miles back to the road.

It was only a temporary victory, however. The canoe was badly damaged and, for all they knew, beyond repair. It was a significant loss to their lifestyle. In addition, their specially made oars from Maine had washed out of the canoe and disappeared downstream.

The possibility of repairing the damage began revolving in Joe's head, even on the ride home. As would become his practice, he lay awake in bed that night trying to figure out the best way to make the necessary repairs. "I started getting ideas and pretty soon I figured out how I might repair it," he explains. "But I didn't have the time to do it in the summer. I thought about that canoe all summer long, but I had to wait until winter before I could start it."

There was no literature or courses in those days, and no canoe factory in the region at which to have the Morris repaired, or even from whom to buy parts. Joe determined he would repair the broken canoe himself, and he was not going to scab together any "Rube Goldberg" patch job that would look odd or be incorrect. Young Joe Seliga would bide his time, and when he did repair the 18-foot B. N. Morris, he would make a first-rate job of it.

Recognition and Respect from Trial and Error

The following autumn, when Joe was cutting firewood outside town, he happened upon a couple of straight cedars and took them down as well, split them, and dropped them off at a mill to be sawn into boards. He then took the boards to the high-school shop, where he milled them into rib stock and planking.

He went home and removed the canoe's canvas skin—still wondering how he would ever stretch on a new piece as tightly—and started removing the broken wooden ribs and planks. Joe recognized that he would have to somehow steam the ribs to make them pliable enough to bend into the correct shapes. He figured his Coleman camp stove could serve as a source of heat, but couldn't decide what to use as a steam chamber. Joe finally settled on an unconventional solution: a length of automobile inner tube tied shut at both ends, with a length of hose channeling steam from water boiling in an old gas can. Today, Joe laughs when he thinks about the contraption that inflated like a fat sausage, and he wonders why he didn't blow himself up in the process or at least scald himself with the pressurized vapor. "But you know," he smiles, "it worked pretty darn good just the same." Using it and working by trial and error, he would eventually make a very good repair on the wooden hull.

Still facing Seliga, though, was the challenge of replacing the canvas, which on a wood-and-canvas canoe is not adhered to the surface of the wood, but rather is stretched tightly around the hull and fastened with tacks along the gunwales and around the curves of the ends. Stretching the heavy material around the complex shape is anything but simple. Joe spent many more nights lying awake pondering, before he finally purchased a length of canvas duck and resolved to go for it. He preshrank the fabric in his mother's washing machine, then fiddled with ways to adequately stretch it around the canoe, finally employing a length of chain twisted taut with an improvised Spanish windlass. The process wasn't without its ups and downs, but it worked well enough. Before Joe was finished, the canvas was as smooth and drum-tight as the original covering.

The canoe companies back East had been developing special compounds to fill the weave of the canvas and make its surface waterproof, paintable, and resistant to abrasion, but the compounds were considered trade secrets and the companies were not about to share their formulas with anyone. Nor were the compounds available in any ordinary hardware store. Recognizing the mildew-resistant properties of white lead, readily procurable in those days, Joe mixed up a concoction of the toxic compound with a measure of linseed oil—a pretty good solution, except that he used raw linseed oil, which forever stays tacky, unlike the boiled version. As a result, the canvas covering on the restored Morris would not last a normal life span, which for such a covering, could be 30 years or more.

Still, after refinishing the new woodwork inside the canoe and painting the exterior, the Morris appeared as good as new and was just as seaworthy, carrying the Seligas into the backcountry for fish, game, and berries. Seliga had a right to be proud. He hadn't rested since the Morris had very nearly met its fate on the Nina Moose. He had pieced together a very cogent plan for making the repairs and thoroughly followed through on each step. The gleaming canoe, once again floating proudly on the surface of Shagawa Lake the following spring, had taught the young craftsman much. Local outdoorsmen were impressed. His efforts would result in welcome extra work fixing other peoples' boats and, in the long run, would lead to a business that would bring Seliga recognition and respect not just in Ely, but everywhere fine canoes were paddled and appreciated.

chapter two

Lesson in Resourcefulness

Joe, with the captain's hat, and his son, Richard, in 1941 with one of Seliga's square-stern "Fisherman" canoes. The popularity of outboard motors like that leaning against the tree in the background led Joe to his initial decision to produce square-stern canoes. *Joe Seliga Collection*

Ely, Minnesota, in the 1930s was a mining town with few opportunities for a young family man. As the Depression held stubbornly to its downward spiral, demand for iron ore, even that as pure as Ely's, was at rock bottom. Although some workers at the nearby Pioneer operation were able to hold onto jobs with reduced hours, neither Oliver Mining nor U.S. Steel was hiring.

The only sure sources of work in the region were federal government's New Deal programs, namely the WPA, CWA, and CCC. While Joe, Nora, and son Richard still occupied the small but comfortable apartment over Joe's parents home on White Street, Joe's older brother Stephen, Jr., had secured a spot at a CCC camp, clearing trails and building bridges in the Superior National Forest. Because of the nature of the work Joe would like to have joined him, but for the time being, the CCC would accept only one member from any family. The WPA was Joe's next option, offering work on federally funded civil programs in towns and cities across the nation. The pay was little, Joe remembers, and the available hours were just 93 per month. It was barely enough to live on.

In addition, the work was strictly manual in nature and of a great variety. "The hardest job I had was digging ditches by hand when they were putting in the town's sewer system," Joe recalls. Later, he was picked to lay forms with the sidewalk-building crew. "That was a pretty good job and lasted quite a while. That sidewalk in front of the house (Joe's current residence purchased in 1950), I laid the forms for it. In fact, I worked on the sidewalks for half the town."

One field in which Joe had distinguished himself, however, was repairing damaged and neglected boats and canoes, of which there was proving to be an abundant supply around Ely. Soon after neighbors had a look at the first-rate repair job Joe had done on the Seligas' damaged B. N. Morris, boats and canoes in need of repairs, canvassing, and refinishing began showing up at his father's garage, which was now pretty much Joe's shop. One local doctor commissioned Joe to make him a pair of oars from sassafras.

"I'd never built any oars," Joe recalls. "But I didn't tell him that," he adds with a chuckle and the trademark gleam in his eye. Joe managed a fine pair of oars, nonetheless, and continued his pattern of "learning on the job" whenever a new problem was presented—which at first seemed like every time someone brought him a neglected canoe.

It was survival by his wits, and a few times Joe had some pretty close calls. One such instance might have resulted in a major fire or serious injuries, but as is often the case, Lady Luck cut the beginner a little slack, and a possible catastrophe became another valuable lesson in what could go wrong. As had become his practice, Joe was using his Coleman stove to heat water in a metal can for steaming a batch of ribs. It was a sizeable job and the two burners, turned up to full capacity, eventually generated enough heat to melt the solder on the stove's fuel tank, sending fuel fumes up into the flame. There was an explosion and Joe felt a sharp pain in his leg. Fortunately, the fuel supply had been nearly exhausted and the resulting fire was not difficult to put out. The pain Joe felt in his leg was the result of the impact from the tank's cap, which blew off in the blast.

It proved not to be a disaster, but serious enough for Joe's father to ban him from doing any more repair work in his garage. "That was it for my father's patience," Joe shakes his head. "He told me he didn't want me burning down the place." Luckily for Joe, his older brother took pity on him, offering his own garage as a place to work. Joe's infant operation moved over a couple of streets to Conan, where it remained until 1952, when Joe built the shop behind his current Pattison Street residence. Seliga's first investment upon moving into Stephen Jr.'s garage was a propane plumber's torch, used to melt lead for fitting pipes, a common practice in those days. It proved safer for firing his steamer than the trusty Coleman camping stove.

A neighbor, Homer Thomas, maintained a fleet of about 10 Old Town canoes that he rented out from a camp on Shagawa Lake. From time to time, Joe would do a little work on one or another of them, and eventually Thomas tried to sell Joe the whole fleet. Though such a purchase was well beyond Joe's financial means, he did manage to purchase one guide's model, which he rented out for a period before reselling it. A few years later he bought three more Old Towns from Thomas' widow and was able to recondition and sell them.

Building the First Seliga Canoe

By 1937, Joe had enough experience to gain a pretty good understanding of how canoes were put together, and he began formulating serious thoughts on the prospect of building his own. At about that time, he wrote to Bert Morris in Veazie, Maine, to inquire about the possibility of becoming a Morris dealer. In 1920, a catastrophic fire had razed the Veazie factory and most of Morris' experienced workers and surviving forms were either at Old Town or Kennebec Canoe in Waterville, Maine. Bert's canoe building had more or less become a hobby and he told Joe that he didn't want to get into a situation where he'd have to fill regular orders.

Joe knew he would need a form of some sort to build cedar-and-canvas canoes like the Morris and Old Towns with which he was familiar. Having seen these forms in the backgrounds of photographs in those manufacturers' catalogs, he knew they were solidly built with metal bands traversing them to clinch the tacks that held the planking to the ribs. Joe figured he could handle such a project, but knew it would take time, a little cash,

Joe and Nora in 1940 with their daughter, JoAnn.
Joe Seliga Collection

and some calculation, all of which he was willing to invest as soon as he could swing it. In the meantime, he explored a second option. Joe already had access to the family's Morris canoes, and with a little ingenuity could make one of them work as a basic shape for constructing a slightly larger canoe with a few modifications of his own.

To begin, Joe decided on a design: a 16-foot double-ended canoe a bit wider than the 15-foot Morris and an inch or so deeper. Using measurements taken and expanded from the existing canoe, he constructed a frame that consisted of pre-bent inwales held in their proper configuration by the thwarts. It was a method commonly used to make birch-bark canoes, which are also built without a mold or form.

Setting this frame aside, Joe bent and prepared a pair of stems with the proper bevel and notches for the anticipated ribs. Next, he temporarily fastened them onto the ends of the 15-foot Morris, extending the stems out 6 inches at each end. Joe then rigged a pair of temporary inwales onto the canoe so he would have something on which to fasten the ribs as they were bent. Then he prepared a set of cedar ribs.

With the Morris canoe, minus its keel, upside down and covered with butcher paper to protect its paint, Joe fired up his steamer and, one by one, bent the hot ribs over the canoe, nailing them to the mock inwales. When the ribs had cured, Seliga lifted the whole unit, stems, ribs, and temporary inwales, from the Morris and secured it right side up to a strongback. The greatest challenge came next when he fit the pre-bent inwales and thwarts he previously set aside to the ribs and stems. "It took a little monkeying," Joe admits, adding, "It convinced me that I would need a real form if I was going to keep doing this."

It was looking good, nonetheless—the curves were fair and the shape pleasing. Joe had a canoe much like the Morris, only longer and deeper.

Planking the skeleton was a big task. Joe had to fit each plank, clamp it in place, and clinch each tack as it was driven, using a variety of steel and iron shapes as clinching irons.

Cow moose on the loose in Ely, October 1988.
Behind the moose is Stephen Seliga's garage, where Joe built his first
canoe in 1937. Joe's childhood home, the White Street house,
is at far right. *Joe Seliga Collection*

Eventually, the planking was satisfactorily accomplished. The canvassing and finishing were steps Joe already knew a thing or two about.

The First Seliga Form

Thus, by 1938, Joe had a pretty 16-foot canoe built, canvassed, cured, and ready to paint. By then, he was already up to his elbows in the second phase of his program: the construction of a bona fide form—this one for a 16-foot square-stern model designed for use with those increasingly popular outboard motors.

Joe spent many nights lying awake in the dark and trying to figure out the best way to build the form and the square stern itself. All he had for reference were the pictures in the big canoe companies' catalogs. Joe finally settled on a style depicted in a well-worn Old Town catalog and figured a 16-foot model like the one illustrated would be popular with fishermen around the Iron Range.

The form's final dimensions would produce a canvas-covered canoe 16 feet long, 40 inches maximum beam, and 14 inches deep with a solid-ash transom. Joe designed its cross-sectional

Charlie's guides Harlan Hanson and Ray Mattson fix a shore dinner during their 1965 voyage from the border lakes of Minnesota to St. Paul. The Seliga canoe they paddled is seen at right.
Photo courtesy The *(St. Paul)* Pioneer Press

I worked at the Sommers Canoe Base from 1961 to 1966. During those years as a guide, I put many miles on several Seliga canoes.

In the fall of 1965, Ray Mattson and I paddled from Moose Lake to downtown St. Paul in a Seliga canoe. We paddled the border lakes to Grand Portage, then down the shore of Lake Superior, up the Brule River to the headwaters of the St. Croix, down the St. Croix to the Mississippi, and back up the Mississippi to the landing in downtown St. Paul. The Brule and the St. Croix were old fur trade routes to St. Louis (we had spent the previous year reading diaries from the historical society). The regional office of the Boy Scouts was about six blocks from that landing, so we portaged to the office. I may still have the newspaper clippings—we were met by the papers and several television stations.

—Harlan Hanson

Joe, his sister Ann, and miscellaneous children take to the water in 1941 aboard one of Joe's square-stern canoes. *Joe Seliga Collection*

patterns, or molds, by modifying the dimensions taken from a large canoe and cutting patterns out of linoleum. He then cut out the cross-sectional molds and set them up along a backbone with plenty of bracing so they wouldn't shift position. Next, Joe milled out full-length spruce strips and ran them along his molds as sheathing, leaving 1/2-inch to 1-inch spaces between them. After fairing the form's shape, he attached straps made from hoop steel about 4 inches on center, over which the ribs would be bent. The steel straps were covered with butcher paper to prevent rust from bleeding onto the steaming wet ribs when they were bent onto the form. As on other forms, Joe's featured recessed backers to support the gunwales, and a channel for the stem at the bow.

Unlike Old Town's square-stern boats, Joe's would not have a wide keelson running along the centerline inside the canoe, requiring the ribs to be prepared and bent full-length rather than in pairs. When building a square-stern, Joe bent an extra-wide rib to support the transom at the stern. The solid transom fit inside the curve of the wide rib and the planking was trimmed flush with the aft surface. A shallow rabbet was cut around the outside surface of the transom and the canvas was pulled around the end of the boat, where it was trimmed to fit neatly into the rabbet and fastened after a good application of bedding compound for a sealant. A good-sized "knee" reinforced the joining of the transom to the bottom of the wide rib, and two additional knees braced the joints between the gunwales and the top of the transom. Joe installed three bench seats, each on its own pair of risers, and a keel along the bottom. On some later versions, Joe added strips along the sides, between the gunwales and the turn of the bilge, to help knock down spray.

It proved a handsome and capable fishing boat, and Joe was correct in predicting it would be popular. In fact, he would go on to build 33 "Fisherman" models, as they eventually came to be known, the last one in 1971. By that time, interest had

> I first paddled a Seliga canoe in 1965 at the Sommer's Canoe Base, but didn't own one until 1977. Since then I've trapped from it, hauled out a moose, gathered rice, and traveled some 8,000 miles in it, through Minnesota, Ontario, Manitoba, and Saskatchewan.
>
> My wife and I have so many wonderful experiences associated with our Seliga that it is hard to imagine what our lives would have been like without it.
>
> —Wayne Lewis

clearly waned, possibly due to restrictions on motors in some nearby wilderness areas. Joe had planned to keep the first one for himself, but even before it was finished a fisherman by the name of Ben Wheat who was visiting from Missouri came by the shop and offered to buy it. "I thanked him, but said, 'No thanks, I think I'll keep this one,'" Joe remembers. But Wheat wouldn't give up, and his persistence paid off. Finally, Joe said to himself, "Hell, why not? I've got the form now, I can always build another one." For years, the large form took up space in one end of the small shop, and was eventually moved to Camp Widjiwagan, where it rests today.

Thus did the first Seliga-built canoe go out the door to Missouri—for $40—and Joe was left standing in his shop with a little cash in his pocket and a bittersweet feeling in his gut. His firstborn canoe was up and gone after months of work and sleepless nights spent puzzling out the form. On the other hand, Joe thought to himself, "Maybe I'll actually be able to sell these things."

Meanwhile, the 16-foot canoe Joe had built over the B. N. Morris also caught the eye of an interested party. This time no cash traded hands, but a neighbor named Joe Kolbe traded Joe a $65 air compressor for the lovely little canoe. In 1938, Depression or not, Joe Seliga was launched into the business of building and selling canoes. It would take a full year working part-time and fitting in repairs before he finished his next square-stern canoe, which was also sold before it was completed, this time to an Ely resident named Eric Walberg. Joe doesn't remember the exact price, only that it was a little better than the first, probably about $60, he guesses. He finished

JOSEPH T. SELIGA
Canoes and Square Stern Canoes

ELY, MINNESOTA

These Canoes, described below, are individually hand made on order only

SPECIFICATIONS OF CANOES

Ribs—White cedar 5/16 inch thick, 2¼ inches wide spaced on 4 inch centers ends tapered.
Planking—White or red cedar 5/16 inch thick smooth laid, long lengths and tight joints.
Stems—Ash or oak, straight grained, steam bent.
Keel—Selected hardwood ⅞ inch depth full length of canoe and well under bang plates.
Canvas—No. 10 seamless duck put on in one piece drawn tight.
Filler—Canvas is made waterproof and smooth with all trace of texture removed by hard drying filler.
Gunwales—Open type which makes washing out much easier.
Seats and Thwarts—Selected hardwood with cane filling, bow seat dropped on 4 in. bolts. Thwarts and stern seat bolted close to gunwales. Two thwarts in the 16' and three in the 18'.
Finish—The hull is completely treated with a preservative and primer inside and out. Three coats of finest Marine Spar Varnish inside. Two coats of Marine paint outside.

Model	Length Extreme	Width Extreme	Depth Amidships	Approx. Weight	Price
Scout	16 ft.	36 in.	12¾ in.	70 lbs.	$170.00
Voyageur	18 ft.	37 in.	13¼ in.	80 lbs.	$178.00
Fisherman Square Stern	16 ft.	40 in.	14½ in.	95 lbs.	$200.00

The Scout and Voyageur models may be had with "Guides Model" lows ends or the higher type as preferred. All models above may be had with a tough nitrate filling at slight additional cost.

The Square Stern is really a fisherman's canoe, very steady, large load capacity and easy to handle. Can be used safely with motors up to and including 5 H. P. In the Scout Model steadiness comes nearly as much from widths as from width and can be entrusted to those who are not accustomed to handling watercraft. The Voyageur has exceptional paddling qualities, and is unusually speedy, can be used with comfort and safety.

A down payment of 25% is required on order, balance on delivery. Prices subject to change when advisable. All quoted are at Ely, Minn.

There is only one Quality in these Canoes—THE BEST.

A 1946 Joe Seliga price sheet. *Joe Seliga Collection*

Joe conducts a seminar in basic canoe repairs for a group of interested Sommers counselors during the late 1950s.
Allen Rench Collection

It was the summer of 1970 that I was first introduced to the wonders of a Seliga canoe. I was taking my first real canoe trip at the age of 14 through the Quetico Provincial Park and BWCAW with my family. We were headed south from Atikoken, Ontario, to Sommers Canoe Base on Moose Lake near Ely.

My father first started bringing scouts to the Sommers Canoe Base in 1956 from Oklahoma. In 1963, after one of these trips, my brother became a guide there. It was my brother's insistence to not paddle a metal canoe on our family canoe trip. The sleek, green, wood-and-canvas craft fascinated me and eventually hooked me forever. It did not take long to see why my brother made it his canoe of choice. He was out ahead in a flash; his track was straight even in quartering crosswinds. When portaging, you were able to enjoy the sounds of the forest rather than the overwhelming screech of branches over an aluminum hull. It wasn't until five years later, while I spent my time guiding Boy Scouts, that I got my chance to enjoy the pleasures of paddling one of Joe's creations. Since then, my father, brother, and I have acquired a number of his canoes to repair and own, and we have cherished each and every one. They have been our shelters, our transportation, and in some way an extension of who we are.

I have felt quite privileged to be able to stop in from time to time and sit with Joe. But more often than not, a simple visit turns into an excursion into history and his craft. I could call Joe up in the dead of winter and ask for a rib or some other part and without question it would be in the mail in short order. No matter who you are, he finds a way to make you feel welcome and like a close friend. He has taught me the value of love for your work and putting your heart and soul into whatever you do. He is one of the most successful and influential men I have ever known.

From my eyes, Joe's worth has never been about his bank account but the relationships that he created through his craft, his devotion to family, and his love of his wife. Because of his works of art, he has enabled my family and countless others to enjoy the wilderness in ways that no other can. Each and every one of his canoes carries Joe and Nora within it. In that way, none of us who paddles one of his canoes are very far from a dear and trusted friend.

—J. Allen Rench

In one of the few modern photographs of the model, Joe's son-in-law Jan Nilsen and grandson Christopher pose with a later Seliga square-stern canoe in 1995. *Joe Seliga Collection*

his third canoe that same year, another square-stern that he managed to hold onto and use for more than a decade, finally trading it in for some accessories on a new Chevrolet he bought in 1950. Ironically, it would be the only period of his life when he actually owned one of his own canoes.

In 1941, Joe built and sold three canoes: two 16-foot square-sterns and another that would prove to be an anomaly in the Seliga line—a 17-foot double-ender. Joe built it over the 15-foot Morris but this time extended the stems even farther past the ends of the original. He built it as a special order for another neighbor, Les Cherne, and charged $75 for it. Joe and Nora, along with their one-year-old daughter, JoAnn, were still living in the upstairs apartment of the White Street house. Joe was unable to find a job in the mines or elsewhere, but the family was managing.

That same year, events in Europe and Asia were awakening the Iron Range's slumbering mining industry. The U.S. government was suddenly very interested in supplying resources to the steel industry, and mines began calling back workers who had been laid off years before and hiring anyone else capable of hard work. Seliga was hired by Pickands-Mather's Zenith operation located off Miner's Lake alongside the other shafts. His job was to sprint along the scaffolding above the rail line and trip the ore-laden hoppers that dumped their loads into waiting railroad cars. "You had to be quick," Joe says, adding with a laugh, "I wouldn't want to have that job now." Joe's job also involved taking ore samples from each carload and putting them in cans that were sent for analysis onsite. Starting pay was $5.25 a day, Joe recalls, with plenty of overtime. In 1944 he remembers earning $1,944, certainly a lifetime high up to that point. He had never felt so rich in his life.

World War II struck Ely as hard as it did any American community, and the men in town were quick to answer the call to arms. Over 1,600 residents (35 percent of Ely's total population) served in the armed forces during the war, one of the highest per capita totals in the nation. However, the community paid a heavy price for its patriotism. The Seliga family was no different than most—Joe's younger brother, Daniel, did not return home alive from central Europe.

Already 30 years old when the U.S. declared war, Joe was not as prime a candidate as younger men. But with a low draft number of 87 he probably would have been called eventually had his job at the mine not qualified him, like many of his co-workers, for deferment. It was a time for buckling down and working hard to quench the war machine's insatiable appetite for iron with which to make steel. Little time and thought were expended on such trivial matters as canoes and outdoor recreation.

As it was, materials like brass fasteners, canvas, quality paints, and good lumber became unavailable overnight. Additionally, with the rationing of gasoline, few sportsmen were driving to the north country. As had happened with the Depression, Joe's efforts to begin a new phase of his life were again thwarted by world events over which he had no control. Other than a little repair work, the Seliga canoe-building enterprise was dead in the water—there are no new canoes listed in Joe's records for the years 1942 through 1945.

Rekindling a Business

The postwar period represented a new era for Nora and Joe and others like them. It was the first time in their lives that peace and relative prosperity came hand-in-hand. Joe was able to keep his job at the Zenith Mine, and suddenly folks could purchase items that had been rationed luxuries during the war—butter, eggs, cigarettes, fresh meat in any quantity, appliances, and gasoline. As the nation restructured its economy for peacetime priorities, men and women who had worked through the war without vacations, and discharged veterans who had spent months or even years overseas, were ready to consider a little recreation.

As necessary materials became available again, Joe wasted little time putting his shop back into operation. He owned but one piece of machinery at the time, a Sears table saw that dated back to the 1930s. It was the first saw with a tilting arbor that the retailer ever offered, and it had previously belonged to a former Winton sawmill owner. Joe purchased it around 1940 for the then-hefty sum of $50—a $40 down payment earned from the sale of a canoe and another $10 installment later on. Remarkably, it is the same table saw in Joe's shop today, more than 650 canoes later. With the war over, Joe was able to swap the saw's original 3/4-horsepower motor for a larger but still "swamped," or trained, at the Sommers Boy Scout Base in 1974. I could only watch with longing and envy as experienced guides headed in or out in those beautiful green Seligas. I might get to help paint or patch or varnish one, but I wouldn't take one out for two years.

In '76, I finally got my own Seliga and felt like a real "Charlie's guide." She was from the bottom of the pile and in desperate need of repairs, paint, and varnish. I splinted her broken gunwale and applied paint and varnish and elbow grease—lots of elbow grease. I was in love. I was dragging her gently over a high beaver dam that summer when I saw a lovely single bloom of iris among the sticks glowing in the morning mist. I knew then her name was *Iris*.

I paddled her for three summers then returned on the fourth to find her gone! She'd been sold. Broke my heart. I have a daughter named Iris now.

My next Seliga didn't even get a name... until I took her to New Orleans with fellow guide Chuck Pease in 1978. We went by way of the entire Mississippi River—2,552 miles. The "experts" said, "Don't take a wooden boat, take a durable aluminum canoe." We knew better. Only a boat as fast and stable and deep, not to mention as pretty, as a Seliga would do the job. In just two hours, we surfed across 14 miles of Lake Winnebegosh with 4-foot rollers! In a Grumman, we would have been forced to swim. We called the Seliga the *Kolodji Queen* and we composed songs to her. She was our home. She was our salvation. She was our ambassador. Her uniqueness and beauty bought us many showers and meals along the way. Dave Byrd of Cincinnati took her home. I wonder if she still has that oil stain at her water line.

I could never hope to buy even a used Seliga from the Sommers Base, so I married a woman who owned one. My wife Doris and her brother bought a Seliga from the Base in 1976. He was handy and fixed her up nicely. Doris guided for the Girl Scouts, named her boat *Dancer*, and kept her on the water. In 1998, I re-canvassed her and painted her purple for Doris's fortieth birthday. It's pretty on the water...like an iris.

—Cory "Godfrey" Kolodji

---

modest 1-1/2–horsepower version, making it easier to re-saw planking stock. "The 'new' motor made all the difference, I can tell you that," Joe says with obvious pride, as though the conversion was made last week instead of 55 years ago. "It's got plenty of wallop, and you could re-saw cedar on it all day long if you wanted to."

Joe also treated himself to a Boyce-Crane thickness planer, a necessary item for ensuring the consistent dimensions of all components, especially since nearly all the lumber bought was rough-sawn from the mill. The Boyce-Crane served Joe and Nora until a shop fire in 1994 melted an irreplaceable part. Clearly, Joe is not the type of woodworker to buy every new gadget on the market. With a full-time job in the mines and weekends reserved for family outings, hunting, and fishing, much of his shop time would have to be during the evenings after work.

With the experience of the square-stern form behind him, Joe forged ahead to build a true form for an 18-foot double-ended canoe. His basic model was the 18-foot B. N. Morris, but he decided to modify its somewhat romanticized lines and produce a canoe a bit more practical for traveling and fishing. To accomplish this, he lowered the graceful but rather high ends a couple of inches, softened the sharp entry to allow it to better ride up on swells, and relaxed the incurving "tumble-home" sides just a bit. Using pine and basswood strips as sheathing, Joe assembled a truly handsome form. He girdled the shape in heavy, 16-gauge galvanized steel bands to reduce bouncing when the brass tacks were driven through the planking and to clinch them tightly on first impact. The first canoe to come off the new form, months after the project had begun, was as striking as Seliga had hoped and exactly what his friend, Bob Binger, had in mind. Binger was a counselor at Camp Widjiwagan, a YMCA camp on the north arm of Burntside Lake. A local outfitter liked it, too, and ordered three more. To round out a good year in 1946, Seliga built two square-sterns and five more in 1947, but no double-enders.

Even before the war, summer camps with canoeing programs had begun springing up in the country outside of Ely. The region's lakes, rimmed both with Canadian shield outcroppings and sandy beaches, and topped by majestic stands of red and white pine, provided an ideal atmosphere for programs designed to get city kids into the fresh air and teach them outdoor skills and respect for the environment. Backed by the endless mosaic of waterways that stretched all the way to Hudson's Bay, it was

Previous pages: Three of the 16-foot Seligas that Joe built on the beefed-up 15-foot Morris he modified for use as a form in 1937 are now at Camp Widjiwagan outside of Ely.

> One of my trips as a guide out of Sommers Wilderness Canoe Base was made memorable by an unfortunate injury to a young Explorer Scout. We were on lay-over on Kawnipi, I think, cooking big ones on a custom-built rock fireplace with a view.
>
> A broken leg meant transport was impossible. Before the days of radios, we had to paddle for help. Luckily, I had a good strong young swamper for a bow man, and we chose the 1959 model Seliga, 20 or 30 pounds lighter, if not faster, than my ancient waterlogged Old Town. We headed for the base at nightfall, a non-stop moonlight race. I recall the night sounds: otters frolicking in front of us at one point…and few words. Got to base for a late breakfast and called for airplane rescue.
>
> A great Seliga made it easier. Thanks, Joe!
>
> —Roger Clapp

also an ideal staging area for programs that organized far-ranging expeditions for its more experienced campers. Central offices in the Midwest's larger cities managed many of the camps.

More importantly for canoe builders, these camps represented a large market. Many of the camps purchased their fleets from established companies back East, like Old Town and Chestnut in New Brunswick, Canada, as well as from more regional builders, like Thompson in Peshtigo, Wisconsin. At first, most of these camps didn't suspect that a part-time builder in a garage right in Ely would soon play a large role in supplying quality canoes ideal for their use.

Camp Widjiwagan, or "Widji" as it's more commonly known, is an arm of the St. Paul, Minnesota YMCA, and was the first area camp to consider such a possibility. After Seliga repaired several of their canoes, two staffers visited Joe in his shop in 1947 and were impressed with the workmanship in the 18-foot double-ender that Joe had begun calling the "Voyager." They were afraid, however, that it was a little large and heavy to be handled safely by their young campers. It didn't take Joe long to assure them that he could produce a 16-footer that would be just the ticket. With an order in hand for several 16-foot canoes, Joe turned back to the 15-foot Morris. He'd proven that he could build a 16-footer over the canoe itself, but he really didn't want to go to all of the trouble he encountered the first time around.

Joe had a solution and began modifying the little canoe, which was ready for some rehabilitation anyhow. First, he removed part of the original stems to provide a stem channel exactly as on his real form. Then he reinforced the lightly built hull with a combination of steam-bent and sawn-to-shape inserts that augmented a temporary backbone on the inside. Next, Joe sheathed the outside with metal bands for clinching the tacks and built Widjiwagan their first four Seliga canoes—16-footers built on the reworked Morris. The camp staff couldn't have been more pleased. He built four more 16-footers that same year, 1948, for another YMCA camp in Des Moines, Iowa. Then, in 1949, Joe built eight for Camp Northland, a girl's camp outside of town, and three more for Widji. The same year, his third child, Nancy, was born.

The eight canoes built for the Northland camp taught Joe a good lesson in testing new products before putting them into regular use. From the start of his business, Joe had experimented with various ingredients in his quest to develop the ideal canvas filler. He seemed to be making progress until he accidentally discovered a commercial product that claimed to be everything he had been looking for. Since it was not terribly expensive and a lot less trouble than mixing his own filler, he ordered a supply just in time for the canoes he was building for the camp. The canoes hadn't been at Northland very long before small cracks began to appear on their painted surfaces. By the end of the season, it was becoming serious. Apparently, the filler had shrunk, causing what's commonly referred to as an "alligator" pattern. Though the filler eventually stabilized, the damage had already been done. Seliga ended up taking each canoe back to his shop, scraping off their paint, refilling their surfaces, and repainting them.

As well as a lesson on adequate testing, it was an affirmation of Joe's no-nonsense guarantee policy. The integrity of a craftsman who stood behind his work would help the young builder establish a reputation that would prove invaluable.

I had the privilege of taking two of Joe's boats on a Widji Voyageur trip in 1978. Starting just above the Saskatchewan border, we headed north and east into the barren lands to the valley of the Thelon, finally heading west to Great Slave Lake via the Mary Frances River and Pikes Portage, finishing at the Dene village of Snowdrift (now known as Lutselke).

We crossed the height of land five times and had lots of long portages, including a particularly brutal nine-mile jaunt up the Mary Frances. It was one of the coldest summers on record, and I remember waking up to find almost a quarter inch of ice on the water pot outside our tent on August 17. Understandably, we all felt low at times, and Joe's boats were a little slice of home that lifted our spirits and kept us moving. The third boat, a synthetic, was small and cold by comparison. Although lighter on the portages, it didn't track as well on the open water of the big lakes and lacked the extra freeboard. The roominess of the wooden boats led us to fight over who would get to paddle them on any given day, and when it was sunny, the ribbed interiors would set off a warm glow. I have a particularly fond memory of paddling down Artillery Lake, everything bathed in the rosy pink twilight of the arctic evening that was reflecting off the woodwork.

Although heavy, Joe's canoes were extremely well balanced and portaged quite nicely, and I was amazed at how the planking in the hull held up, still stiff after years of service. In fact, I bet those boats are still transporting eager young adventurers through the lake country of the northern Ontario wilderness.

—Erik Hobbie

Long before Joe's son Richard was old enough to help out, Joe had put "& Son" on the decals that adorned his canoes' decks. As work in the canoe shop increased, however, and Dick reached high school, he began helping out in earnest. It was good part-time employment for a teenager, and the young Seliga picked it up quickly. After high school, Dick studied drafting at Ely Junior College and continued helping out until 1951, when he joined the Army. Because Joe continued working full time at the Zenith Mine, Dick's help provided a welcome boost to the operation.

Establishing a Reputation

In at least three ways, 1950 proved to be an important year for Seliga. Since building the first 18-footer for Bob Binger, Joe was a little uneasy with its size. Many of the region's backcountry portages wound through heavy stands of timber and outcroppings; getting around all the corners was tricky with an 18-foot canoe on your shoulders. Joe, who knew this from experience, began hearing it from others. Also, with youngsters regularly using Seligas at area camps, Joe recognized the attraction of a slightly shorter canoe. He already had a method of making 16-footers with the 15-foot Morris as a mold, but he didn't want to alienate serious fishermen by going too small, so he settled on 17 feet and went about rebuilding the ends of his 18-foot form to accommodate the compromise. At the same time, Joe made one final change to the B. N. Morris' styling, further softening the sharp rise of the sheer at the bows. Though it was a beautiful thing to look at on the Morris, it was not always practical on big and sometimes windy lakes.

Joe had a canoe that really suited him, yet preserved a bit of the heritage of the beloved Morris. Seliga would reflect these roots in his lifelong attention to the details on each and every canoe he would build. "The Veazie canoe was the best," Joe emphatically states. "That's what they called the Morris canoes around here—the Veazie canoe. They looked the best and, oh boy, the workmanship was perfect. Everywhere in the canoe you could see it. I tell you, B. N. Morris had a damned fine crew working for him."

Joe's standard canoe from that point on would measure 17 feet in length with a beam amidships of 36 inches and an inside depth of 13 inches. It represents about 90 percent of all his canoe output and is the model he builds today.

The second major occurrence in 1950 was the couple's purchase of a home of their own: a modest but handsome two-story affair on a large lot at the corner of Third and Pattison. Well-built and maintained, it provided plenty of space for the family, and Nora kept it sparkling clean, nicely decorated, and, above all, homey. There was also room for a respectable garden and, even more exciting to Joe, space to build a large shop of his own, although this wouldn't come about until

1952. In the meantime, Joe and his father moved a small garage onto the property, principally for storage.

The third event of 1950 that would have lasting impact on Joe's career was the start of a mutually beneficial relationship with the Charles L. Sommers Wilderness Canoe Base (since 1988 called Northern Tier High Adventures), located 22 miles east of Ely and just outside the BWCAW on Moose Lake. Started in 1923 and run by the Boy Scouts of America, the Sommers Base began as a program to get Boy Scout troops from northeastern Minnesota out into the surrounding wilderness of the BWCA and Ontario's Quetico Provincial Park—and safely back again. For 18 years the program had no permanent base of its own, running its trips from existing lodges or other suitable starting spots. Word got around nonetheless, and soon troops from the entire Midwest were taking advantage of the service, which provided group gear, canoes, and guides. The base camp on Moose Lake opened in 1941 and was named for St. Paul businessman Charles Sommers, a financial supporter of the base. Before long, Scouts not just from northeastern Minnesota and the Midwest, but from all over the United States, were being led through the border lakes by "Charlie's guides," as the mostly college-aged trip leaders were nicknamed.

In 1949, staff members from Sommers had visited Seliga and, learning that he planned to replace the handsome 18-foot Voyager with a 17-foot model, promptly ordered several for the next season, as well as one 18-footer with a "V" stern to accommodate a small outboard. The following year, Sommers bought 10 more canoes and indicated they planned to do so each year in the foreseeable future.

Seliga had to do some figuring. These were some serious orders, but Joe doubted that canoe building would provide enough income on its own, even with this new market. "Heck," he says, "in those days I was lucky to break even. There was no way I could quit my job at Zenith, and still support the family."

chapter three

Recipe for the Good Life

Joe displays one of his newly crafted canoes just outside his backyard workshop in the 1970s. *Courtesy Bob Cary*

If 1950 was marked by three landmark events in Joe's career as a master canoe builder, in 1951 a single event occurred that would trump all three. Building a dozen canoes a year is a lot of work, especially on top of a full-time job. When Richard entered the Army in 1951, leaving Joe alone in the shop, it proved the ideal opportunity for Nora to quietly work her presence into the building routines. At first it was just to neaten things up or to hold a plank while Joe fit it and drove a few tacks. However, in no time, Nora could be found opposite Joe on the other side of the form, taking one end of a hot rib, holding it flat against the bottom, expertly bending it around the metal band, and nailing its end to the inwale.

Nora became an expert nailer, as well. Joe would fit a plank, attach it in place with a couple of tacks, and move on to another while Nora drove the remaining 30 or 40 tacks necessary to secure the piece. "There's not a woman anywhere who's driven anywhere near as many tacks as Nora has," Joe claims with obvious pride. The couple became a real team in the shop, as well as in life. By the time their daughter Nancy started school in 1954, Nora was varnishing the canoes while Joe was at Zenith. She also kept all the records and handled all correspondence. It would not have been a viable operation without Nora's efforts. Besides preparing the family's meals, Nora also provided tens of thousands of fresh donuts and muffins and gallons of hot coffee for the customers, onlookers, camp counselors, game wardens, and eventually the pilgrims who streamed through the Seligas' shop, their kitchen, and their lives. Everyone seemed to be realizing that when you bought a Seliga canoe, or even just admired one, you became part of an extended family and made friends for life.

Nora's loving attention and unselfish help never went unnoticed, least of all by Joe. "I never heard her complain about the work and time that a family requires," Joe states. "She got the children off to school each day of the school year. She got up early and made my breakfast and lunch pail, and saw me off to work. When I went fishing for a weekend with my buddies, she was home to greet me when I returned. She'd take my pack, take out the fish, and refrigerate them immediately, hang my clothes and sleeping bag on the clothesline, and by the time I had cleaned up, she had a meal on the table."

"One Sunday after I had retired from the job at the mine," he continues, "she had gotten up after we had finished eating and started to clean up the pots. I got up and squeezed in between her and the corner of the kitchen counter. I nudged her slowly away from the sink before she could ask me what I was up to. I told her, 'Nora, you have always helped me with many things. From now on, I will wash all the dishes and pots and pans. You can dry them if you want.' I did that for 26-1/2 years."

In the spring of 1952, Joe and a few friends poured the concrete slab that would serve as the foundation for an extra-long, two-car "garage" that would never house a car, but instead would be used as Seliga's canoe shop. Throughout the summer, Joe kept at the project whenever he had the chance, laying the cinder-block walls and framing and sheathing the roof with lumber from the small garage, now dismantled, that he and his father had moved to the property two years before. Joe equipped the shop with two sizable glass-block windows in the back, a single small window and door facing the yard and garden, and wide garage doors on the street end. He also included a loft suitable for storing lumber. It was as simple a structure as might be conceived, but it immediately came to life with the activity of fine canoe building and still serves Joe today.

As Joe had discovered by this time, the bottleneck in wood-and-canvas canoe production occurs during the month or so it takes for the canvas filler to cure before the canoe can be painted. With the Sommers Base knocking on the door and Nora helping out with the work, Joe began looking around for a faster way to meet the growing demand.

New Technology and a Return to Tradition

Like many sportsmen in the 1950s, Seliga was familiar with Herter's of Waseca, Minnesota, a large catalog merchant that sold anything and everything an outdoorsman of the era could want. Rods and reels, rod blanks, fly-tying materials by the ounce and by the pound, duck boats, canoes, compasses, clothing, firearms, turkey calls—Herter's was the Cabela's of their time. The only difference was that Herter's offered a large selection of unique merchandise they claimed to have developed, and they were not shy about describing with extravagant catalog copy. One of the more interesting listings in the 1952 catalog was a line of fiberglass products that included glass cloth, polyester resin, hardeners, and pigments, and which was billed as the panacea for all manner of problems with wooden boats, from checked canvas, to cracked ribs, to raging dry rot. A layer of glass cloth, saturated with the amazing resin and allowed to cure, would make almost any boat or canoe lighter, stiffer, completely waterproof, and so resistant to abrasion that the renewed craft could be depended upon indefinitely. It wasn't only Herter's who sang the praises of this wondrous new technology—seemingly everyone was discovering how simple it was to remove torn or rotten canvas from an old canoe and replace it with a layer of the fiberglass, thus eliminating

Joe restores a Detroit Boat Company canoe in his shop in May 1983.
Joe Seliga Collection

all possibilities of future troubles. Everyone was claiming it was by far tougher than the original canvas.

"Guys were saying you couldn't shoot a hole in it with a .22 rifle," Joe remembers with a wry smile. "I never believed that, of course, but what little I could find to read about it made it sound pretty good."

So, in 1953, Joe took the bait. He ordered some glass cloth and resin and went to work applying a layer of cloth to a new canoe hull instead of canvassing it. It was not nearly as foolproof as he'd been led to believe. "It was awful stuff, especially in those days," Joe explains. "It was so sticky you got it all over yourself, and the smell was terrible. You never knew if it was going to harden or not. Sometimes it would harden on one part of the canoe, but on the other side it was as sticky as when you put it on. And the tiny fibers, when you went to sand the stuff, I tell you there's nothing more itchy than that."

Joe wrestled with the foul-smelling resin, which tended to ball up the cloth while the roller melted in the pan. Plus, the new shop stank of styrene instead of cedar, and the cured cloth was riddled with nearly invisible pinholes that allowed water to seep into the canoe. Although Joe had plenty of reasons to abandon the idea after the first couple of canoes, by experimenting, paying attention, and asking a few questions, he started to get the upper hand and felt he might actually tame the beast. Once he mastered a few tricks, the canoes began looking presentable. What's more, it didn't take any longer than canvassing and filling, the cost was comparable, and best of all, he didn't have to wait a month for filler to cure.

The result was a leap forward in production, and in 1953 the Seligas built 15 glass-covered canoes for the Sommers Base. The following year, they produced an incredible 20 17-footers, plus five additional canoes and square-sterns for individual customers—all of them sheathed in fiberglass, as well. It was a punishing year, and it became clear to Joe and Nora

Joe and his friend, Kevin Timoney, in 1981, at Dorset, Ontario, where the Seligas were attending an assembly of the Wooden Canoe Heritage Association (WCHA). Naturally, they're paddling a Seliga. *Joe Seliga Collection*

> I met Joe and Nora in the early-1980s and was amazed by the beauty of their canoes. So I started saving my money… someday I hoped to paddle one of my very own. Lucky for me, I met a woman, soon to become my wife, who also enjoyed being out on the water. I proposed to Mary one fall evening on a lake not far from Ely and the next day we were at Joe's shop picking out the color of her engagement canoe. Joe and Nora were the first to know our happy news (even before our parents). To us, a Seliga canoe was a perfect symbol of commitment in marriage, when you think about the love between Joe and Nora.
>
> Also, there is no better boat to handle the big waves (of life) than a Seliga canoe. A few years later, Mary and I were just getting back from a 10-day trip in the BWCAW. We were driving back to Ely on the Fernberg Trail about 15 miles from town when I saw a car that passed us going the opposite direction turn and started to follow us all the way back to Ely. When we stopped in town we saw that it was Joe. He got out of his car with a big smile and came up to us asking how we liked the canoe and the details of our trip.
>
> Like parents recognizing their children—that's how Joe is with his canoes. He saw his canoe go by at 50 miles per hour and he wanted to know how we liked it and if we had treated it kindly, even if it meant following us all the way back to town.
>
> —Joseph Bianco

that the fun went out of canoe building when they took on too much. "Oh boy, was I getting growly," Joe says of the toll the added workload began to take.

There had been little time for family, friends, themselves, berrying, fishing, and all the other activities that made life at the edge of the wilderness appealing. Joe and Nora vowed they would never let it happen again. Seliga settled into a production rate of 12 to 15 canoes per year. With the new shop, and Nora's help, it was manageable and Joe could still grab an occasional weekend to catch walleyes or ice fish for lake trout.

Throughout the 1950s, nearly every canoe that passed through the shop door went to Sommers and other camps. In fact, 1959 was devoted to a new project brought about by a request from the directors of the Plymouth Youth Center of Moorhead, Minnesota, and Minneapolis, who expressed interest in a 17-foot canoe made of solid fiberglass, not wood sheathed in fiberglass, like those built for Sommers. The Plymouth directors were convinced it was the way of the future, and in fact Joe had been giving such fabrication some thought himself. He determined it would involve making a hollow, fiberglass mold using a canoe as a "plug," since fiberglass canoes are laid up inside a two-piece mold, rather than built on the outside of a form like wooden canoes.

It was a challenge and an opportunity. Joe has always been receptive to both, so he agreed to the project, producing a mold and nine all-fiberglass 17-footers, the entire year's production. Joe's heart wasn't in it, however, and the canoes lacked the beauty and life of their cedar-and-canvas counterparts. Joe was also concerned about the effects of the fumes and airborne fibers. "If people had seen me walking into the house from the shop after working with that stuff," he says of the fumes, "they would have thought I was a drunk."

So, almost as quickly as it began, the experiment ended. Seliga kept the mold around, but used it only to produce those nine canoes in 1959. The first two or three of the all-fiberglass canoes produced proved to be a bit light in structural integrity and their bottoms flexed excessively. Joe brought them back to his shop and laid a few transverse "ribs" made of resin-saturated heavy "roving" glass cloth across their bottoms. This seemed to stiffen them substantially and he put them in the subsequent fiberglass canoes. What ultimately happened to these nine unique canoes is anyone's guess.

The year prior, the Zenith Mine had closed and the other operations in Ely were not hiring. Some of Joe's co-workers took jobs at a taconite-producing facility 60 miles to the south, in the town of Aurora. Local workers nearing retirement commuted, while others relocated. Joe and Nora, however, could not bear the idea of pulling up stakes and leaving Ely, and their hesitation paid off. Soon, the Captive Mining Corporation took over the old Zenith facility and Joe was back to work as a hoisting engineer—a better job than he had before the closing, with plenty of overtime as well. As hoisting engineer, Joe manipulated the huge

Joe and Nora at Burntside Lake in 1988 amid a fleet of their canoes, all of which belong to the family of Larry Coppola. *Joe Seliga Collection*

Joe and Nora bend ribs around the form in the shop. *Joe Seliga Collection*

I had wanted a Seliga canoe since I was a Widji camper. My husband never believed me when I explained how nice they are—he is the drag-the-aluminum-canoe-around type! Then he did a building job for one of the Widji's past directors and noticed the Seliga in his garage.

Dale was able to fly up to Ely several times while the canoe was in the process of being built, so we have pictures of the construction process. He was also able to bring some ash that he and my father-in-law logged and milled on our land for Joe to use on my canoe. I think that he used some of it for the seats and thwarts.

The finished canoe was a birthday surprise several years ago. It was a huge surprise, since I had heard a rumor many years earlier that Joe was no longer making canoes! When we picked it up, we had Joe sign his name on the inside, as a true artist would.

Dale has since discovered that he does like wooden canoes. He no longer thinks that they would be clunky and hard to paddle and is constantly impressed with the quality, workmanship, and beauty of Joe's canoes. Right now it is one of the main focal attractions in our living room, where we have it hanging on the wall.

—Kari & Dale Juntunen

Joe inspects the bottom of one of his canoes at the 1986 WCHA Assembly in Paul Smiths, New York. That's a B. N. Morris behind him.
Joe Seliga Collection

> I used to be a "Charlie's guide" 20 years ago. During my second summer at Sommers Canoe Base, I was so lucky to be able to go out on a 10-day trip in a Seliga canoe. It was my longest trip that summer, and I remember the first portages—they were tough.
>
> On the first day I took my crew up to Louisa Falls, which required four portages. I guess that I was kind of tired that night, but to paddle that canoe, that was something else. The way it was riding the waves and gliding through the water was just so beautiful. It was a lot faster than those Grumman canoes my crew was paddling. After a few days I forgot all about the weight. It was so well-balanced to portage—one hand in the pocket and the other one on the gunwale.
>
> Since my days at the base, I have done quite a few canoe trips in the Northwest Territories and in the Yukon, and lots of paddling here in Scandinavia and in Scotland. But the Seliga is the best canoe I have paddled.
>
> —Torben Bruhn Andersen
> Copenhagen, Denmark

drums and cables that lifted both workers in their "car" and ore cars up and down the shafts. On a bell signal, Joe would "pop it in gear, give it the juice, and watch the dial that told me when to slow it down." The signals were one, two, or three bells, Joe explains, "so you wanted to be sure to stay awake, so you knew which one."

But staying awake wasn't always so easy—often Seliga worked two shifts. The financial end of it, though, made it worth his while. "It was the first time I could reach in my pocket and pull out a dollar bill," he joked. "Before that, the only things in my pockets were holes." The job lasted just over three years, just long enough for the picture to improve at Reserve Mining in nearby Babbit. At 16 miles, it was a reasonable commute.

At Reserve, Seliga was first placed in the general labor pool and worked anywhere help was needed, but he was soon moved into the railroad department's repair facility, a large, well-equipped shop where railroad cars were completely overhauled. His first job in the shop involved inspecting wheels for cracks. It turned out to be an interesting, stress-free place to work, and Joe stayed with it for 13 years until he retired in 1976 at age 65.

By 1960, Seliga had grown tired of covering his canoes with fiberglass cloth and wary of its supposed benefits. Canoes sheathed in the stuff looked great when they went out the door, but later exhibited noticeable problems. Some developed hairline cracks as the glass grew more rigid with age. It was also apparent that the glass straightjackets prevented the cedar from flexing naturally when the canoe came up against resistance, resulting in cracked ribs and planking where there otherwise wouldn't have been any. Worst of all, the planking developed dry rot wherever the sheathing failed and water got in, and the impermeable coating made it difficult to dry out. Still another problem surfaced when it came time to repair a damaged canoe: the fiberglass bonded to the planking well enough to make it very difficult to remove, often tearing out plank fibers with it.

The evidence was troublesome enough to Joe for him to turn back to the old way, and in 1964 he covered his last canoe with fiberglass and has remained faithful to the traditional canvas ever since.

Pilgrimage to the Mecca of Canoe Building

A road trip in 1967 proved especially memorable for Joe and Nora. After more than 30 years of building his own canoes, Joe finally had the chance to visit one of the world's premier canoe-building companies. Located in the eastern Maine city for which it was named, Old Town Canoe Company had its start before the turn of the century. The Seligas managed to get a guided tour of the immense brick facility, which was still building mostly canvas-covered canoes and cedar-planked, lap-strake powerboats, although one floor of the plant was already converted over to production of all-fiberglass craft.

Joe had followed Old Town's catalogs most of his life, and viewing the forms in person and being in the midst of the history was a genuine thrill. It was his first real look at how the manufacturers did things, and it proved a resounding confirmation of his own ingenuity and craftsmanship. Joe could see how Old Town's forms and jigs were built and watched carefully as the various building steps were performed. He was amazed by how close he had come on his own, with no formal experience or training. He recognized places where his methods differed, but for the

Joe shows the famous Seliga grin. And no wonder—these lake trout will provide some good eating. *Joe Seliga Collection*

most part Joe was satisfied with his unique solutions. "Of course I learned a few things, too," Joe admits. "I learn something, it seems, in just about every shop I visit." Joe Seliga had always felt his product compared favorably with that of the best manufacturers—once again, his confidence was reaffirmed.

The Seligas also drove through nearby Veazie, Maine, once home of the large B. N. Morris factory that had been destroyed by fire in 1920, just to pay tribute to the pioneer Seliga had always thought of as his mentor. Across the Penobscot River, Joe visited a small, one-man operation whose proprietor, a former Old Town employee, was generous enough to share his filler recipe. The visit to the shop proved worth the entire trip: the concoction became the basis for the successful self-made compound Seliga has used ever since.

Across the border in Canada, a visit to the famous Chestnut Canoe plant in Fredericton, New Brunswick, proved disappointing because the place was all but shut down for a holiday. Joe and Nora got a walking tour of the factory, however, and watched a couple of craftsmen weave snowshoes, the plant's only production that week. Still, in typical Seliga fashion, Joe managed to learn a few things from what he observed passing through, in this case, mostly how Chestnut's production floor was set up.

The Camp Trade

Throughout the 1960s, camps like Sommers and Camp Menogyn, a Minneapolis YMCA camp on northern Minnesota's Gunflint Trail, provided the Seligas with most of their orders. Sales to the camps proved a two-edged sword: not only did the camps buy the capable Seligas in quantity, many of their counselors and even young campers fell in love with them and would end up one day buying one for themselves. Many counselors and former campers also enjoyed visiting the Seligas each year, and more than a few are considered lifelong friends.

In 1972, Sommers Wilderness Base bought their one hundred twenty-second, and final, wooden canoe from the Seligas. While the tremendous growth of their programs made the purchase of aluminum and synthetic canoes seem more practical, it was a sad decision as far as many of Charlie's guides were concerned. As the old canoes were phased out, a common topic of conversation between the experienced guides was the diminished character the trips took on without the venerable wooden canoes. Ultimately, these traditionalists got a form of compensation for the loss. During the 1970s, Sommers put their discontinued Seligas up for sale at very reasonable prices, and staff members got first dibs on the merchandise. Still, it's evident from letters and conversations with former "Charlies" from the 1950s and 1960s that the integrity and beauty of the Seliga canoes furnish some of their fondest memories. Sommers' decision aside, the camp trade otherwise held through the first half of the 1970s, mostly on the strength of Menogyn and a renewed interest by Widjiwagan.

Retirement Opens New Vistas

Joe retired from Reserve Mining in 1976. Enjoying good health and lots of energy, he figured that he and Nora would increase the number of canoes they built each year from the 10 to 12 that had become their average. Instead, Joe found himself relaxing and enjoying his family, including a growing number of grandchildren, more than he had in the past. The couple also went out on more berrying excursions, and Joe increased the frequency of his trips to favorite fishing lakes. (Ironically, since trading in his square-stern in 1950, Joe was still without a canoe of his own, though, to this day, he never has trouble borrowing a canoe from friends, camps, or relatives.) Seliga has also always enjoyed snowmobiling; not the fancy overpowered jobs, which he says he could never afford, but the low-geared simple machines designed for getting into backcountry lakes like those around Ely and in Canada. So instead of the increased production Joe had expected, output remained about the same. And as private individuals overtook the area camps as Joe's largest customer base, he and Nora enjoyed the opportunity to meet more enthusiasts when they came to Ely to pick up their prizes.

Because Joe learned his craft in a vacuum, not to mention the fact he held a full-time mining job in addition to his canoe building, such person-to-person contact with like-minded aficionados and builders from outside the region had been relatively limited. In 1980, he and Nora became charter members of the fledgling Wooden Canoe Heritage Association (WCHA), which has since grown into a worldwide, 2,500-member organization dedicated to the preservation, enjoyment, and promotion of wooden canoes, new and old. The Seligas were occasionally lured to annual WCHA gatherings in locations like Ontario, Maine, and the Adirondacks, where the couple met new canoe enthusiasts who inevitably gravitated to Joe at the events. Joe is still a member of the organization, which counts among its roll many proud owners of Seliga canoes.

Joe Seliga has never overlooked the bounty of the northwoods. Here, he shows off a nice haul of wild cranberries in 1986.
Joe Seliga Collection

However, the canoe-related travel wasn't limited to WCHA events. In January 1989, Joe and Nora were invited to appear as paid exhibitors at a large boat show in Minneapolis' Metrodome. Joe brought both a completed canoe and a bare hull just off the form to putter away at while he talked to interested passersby. He was set up right on home plate where, he takes pleasure in noting, Twins sluggers were thrilling baseball fans of the day. The Seliga exhibit was a big success from the standpoint of the promoters, as well as for Joe, who wrote orders for several new canoes.

Joe's popularity and modest manner did not go unnoticed by the promoter of a similar event in Kansas City, and when Joe expressed some reluctance to attend, the organizers made a generous offer that was difficult to refuse. Joe agreed to go and, to his surprise, Nora decided to accompany him. Once again, Joe and his canoes became an unexpected, folksy center of attention in the convention center packed with hulking fiberglass powerboats. Joe talked to dozens of people who had no idea that wood-and-canvas canoes were still being built. Once again the show was a success from a business standpoint.

The shows were a novel experience, but also distracting, tiring, and, it could be argued, against the Seliga ethos. Joe isn't spinning a sales yarn when he says, "I have never sold a canoe." Rather, Joe has always let the workmanship speak for itself, and customers have always accepted the fact that he is careful not to promise exact completion dates, instead con-

Owner Chuck Rose portages the Seliga he often loans out so that others may experience the joy of paddling one. *Chuck Rose Collection*

My favorite Seliga memory happened the day I got the canoe back after it had been repaired. John (Beltman) had done more than I expected, including refinishing the inside. We met at the Wild Rice Rendezvous that was taking place at a restoration of a Northwest Company fur trade post, outside of Pine City, Minnesota.

In the evening, scores of the participants paddled the lake-like section of river into town. A friend and I left the program just a little early to start paddling back, ahead of the pack. We paddled hard at first, then settled into a smooth rhythm. There was no wind or moon that night, and the like-new canoe moved quietly through the cool darkness. There was just enough starlight so that we could keep the canoe in the center of the river. We could faintly hear ducks and geese moving around on the water. We hardly spoke, afraid to break the spell.

The past two summers, I have loaned my Seliga back to the Sommers Canoe Base so that a new generation of Charlie's guides could share in the experience of paddling a Seliga. I look forward to getting it back during the winter, touching it up, and loaning it out again.

—Chuck Rose

> I call her *Phoenix*. I picked her up two days before my birthday in the early spring of 1996, along with Joe's admonition, "Use, but don't abuse." She was number 96 607 1, Joe's 607th canoe.
>
> While at Joe's shop, I became mesmerized by the random, paint-spattered floor. Having survived the fire, that floor abstractly chronicled the many decades of a canoe builder's fine art. At this auspicious moment, I remember feeling exactly as I had when I held in my hands the artist's palette of Francis Lee Jaques.
>
> *Phoenix's* maiden voyage was shortly after ice-out that year, on the Pine River in Minnesota's Crow Wing County. My ceremonial bow man was Einer R. Anderson. Back when I started at Sommers, each trip was preceded by a mandatory viewing of the film *Wilderness Day*, a memorable production that focused on "pre-nylon" and "pre-aluminum can" canoe camping. We continued to show it at the base long after the changing times called for regular caveats. Einer had been the star of that movie.
>
> Nowadays, we have all but succumbed to path-of-least-resistance lifestyles. As a people, we seem totally enamored of noise, power, speed, and convenience. We have commissioned our institutions, public and private, to insulate us from the uncertainties of wildness and weather, day and night, despite Sig's early warning of inevitable spiritual consequences.
>
> I say, "Raise your paddles to Joe Seliga!" Through his superlative canoes, he's a true enabler and perpetuator of the naked experience of wildness. Those of us who have been so fortunate as to be bared to the Great Weather have so, so often found ourselves, mid-stroke, giving thanks that we were not in a lesser craft.
>
> —Ron Miles

tacting the buyer once when their canoe is started and again when he knows an approximate completion date. With a lengthy waiting list built on the strength of his canoes' reputation, Joe and Nora were able to refuse further invitations to participate in large commercial shows, even though they continued to receive generous offers.

A Serious Fire and a Courageous Rebuilding

In the winter of 1994, Seliga's canoe-building tradition very nearly came to an abrupt end. On the dark and frigid morning of February 10, with the thermometer dipping to minus-30 degrees Fahrenheit, a gusty wind came up early, sending the chill factor even lower. Joe and Nora had finished eating breakfast and Joe headed out to start a fire in the shop's barrel stove. On cold mornings like this, it was Seliga's routine to start a fire in the stove and come back into the house for another cup of coffee while the shop heated up. While lighting the fire, he noticed a damp rag lying on the steam box and set it on top of a stick leaning against the wall behind the stove to dry. On the way out the door, Joe unknowingly dislodged the stick, which toppled against the surface of the stove.

Joe took his time with his coffee to give the barrel stove more time to work. It was Nora who first noticed the funny-colored smoke blowing by outside, which the couple at first dismissed as blowing snow. A closer look out the kitchen window, however, revealed the true cause of the wisps—ugly columns of oily smoke rolling out beneath the shop's eaves.

Joe ran to the shop and pushed open the door. The draft ignited the superheated air inside, causing a flash explosion. Joe was struck on the cheek by flying debris, and his eyebrows were singed. He accidentally knocked over the shop phone hanging next to the door, tying up the line and making it impossible for Nora to call the fire department from inside the house. Several minutes were wasted until a passerby ran to a neighbor and placed the call. The first responders from the firehouse located just a few blocks from Joe's house were alongside the shop in a few minutes, but the fire had gotten a good start, with plenty of good fuel to build on. Inside, flames licked at the form and a couple of canoes that were underway in the middle of the shop. The fire climbed to the ceiling, stretching for the select lumber Joe had stored in the rafters overhead. Despite the cold and the dense smoke that had driven Joe from the shop, the firemen got their pumps started and played water over the dirty orange flames.

Jeanne Bourquin, a longtime friend of the Seligas and a canoe builder who lives across Shagawa Lake from town, was in Ely that morning and heard the sirens. With dread, she spotted the black smoke billowing above Seliga's block and was soon on the scene. Although filled with smoke, the cinder-block shop was still standing, and most of the flames had been extinguished. Bourquin joined others who had opened the end of the loft and

Nora and Joe pause on an early winter walk with their spaniel, Lucky Boy, in 1986. *Joe Seliga Collection*

were pulling out smoldering canoe stock. Joe was neither badly hurt nor panicked or self-pitying. "What he kept talking about," Jeanne recalls, "was how he would change the form if he had to rebuild it."

Fortunately, the form was spared, although it would need some rebuilding. The band saw, the treasured Boyce-Crane planer, handheld power tools, jigs, and, perhaps most tragically, years of records stored in wooden drawers were destroyed. Most of the handles were burned off the hand tools that had belonged to Joe's father. Rafters were scorched and cedar, spruce, and mahogany lumber charred, much of it beyond reclamation. The two new hulls were charred, and the canvas of another canoe ruined by the heat. Also burned was the irreplaceable pair of spoon oars that his father had purchased with the big Morris. Almost precisely 60 years earlier, they had been swept from the stricken canoe, swamped on the Nina Moose River. Two years later, they were miraculously recovered downstream and returned to the Seligas. Now they were burned beyond hope. The shop was a blackened, sooty mess. Cardboard and wooden containers holding tacks, nails, nuts, and bolts had burned, spilling their contents onto the floor where the metal was coated with a slurry of frozen soot and water.

It could have been worse, but it was plenty bad enough. The larger tools were taken to Bourquin's shop for appraisal, cleaning, and when possible, repair. Widjiwagan's manager, Joe Smith, another of Joe's close friends, took the blackened canoes and damaged lumber to the Widji shop, along with the old reinforced 15-foot Morris and the fiberglass mold Joe used to build fiberglass canoes for the Plymouth Youth Center in 1959. At Widji, the staff worked to salvage something useful from the remains.

Joe and Nora were disheartened, but not ready to quit. Other than planning, there wasn't much that could be done with the frozen mess over the rest of the winter.

All of Joe and Nora's grandchildren have been given Seliga canoes. Here, the grandparents launch the one built for Alison Richards in 1987. *Joe Seliga Collection*

In 1989, Joe took one completed canoe and one in-progress canoe to Minneapolis for a sport and boating show at the Metrodome. *Joe Seliga Collection*

Joe on a 1990 canoe trip with his friend, Dan Litchfield. *Joe Seliga Collection*

Nora and Joe picked these wild blueberries in 1990 near Lake Jeannette on the Echo Trail. Berry picking was a common activity for Joe and his siblings when they were growing up in Ely, just as the Echo Trail was a frequent hunting and fishing haunt. *Joe Seliga Collection*

When at last spring rolled around, a group of friends helped Joe rip out the worst damage. His neighbor, Mike Braun, brought over a pressure washer and started cleaning the oily black film that clung to every surface. Then Joe himself took over the formidable chore of rebuilding. Rafters were replaced or reinforced, benches rebuilt, new insulation installed, and sections of the roof replaced. Fasteners that had spilled onto the floor were collected and sorted by Nora and washed clean with a toothbrush. "Materials like this were covered by the insurance," Joe explains, "But Nora just couldn't stand to see all these good brass bolts and stuff thrown out."

Tools were replaced, the bands on the form reset, and every surface scrubbed until there was no trace of the blaze. By September, Joe and Nora were back in the shop building canoes.

Since the fire, many of the canoes built in Joe's shop have been for the last few grandchildren who haven't already received one, although a few are built each year for special

My most outstanding or unusual Seliga story was the day I dropped *Kathy*. We were coming out of Sarah Lake to the southwest, on the second portage out of her, maybe 200 meters long. There was a pretty little stream with a waterfall, rapids, and pool at the far end.

As I came to the end of the portage, it got a bit steep. It had rained the day before. My right foot hit a patch of slick blue clay, and started skating. "No problem," my reflexes flashed. "Just lift up the other foot and ski down a bit." But the other foot had slipped forward about 2 inches and the toe of my boot was under a rock overhang. I tried to lift it and it stuck. Right foot going forward, left stuck under a rock, me doing the splits. I did not, however, drop the boat then. I was a third-year guide, by God, and was not going to be abusing the base equipment, much less a prime Seliga!

Well, the right leg landed on a rock, just below the knee. It had all 160 pounds of me, 40 pounds of guide's pack, and 130 pounds of *Kathy* on top of it. The impact was one of those experiences you only have a few times in your life, really a deep shock. WHAM! And then it went numb. As I went back up and started back down, my reflexes decided that the base's honor was not worth a compound fracture, and I rolled the boat off.

When it hit, it made a noise like you would expect if you were to jump off a roof onto a case of cornflakes. CRRUNCCHHH. I was sure my leg was broken, because of the numbness, but it was not as things turned out. The *Kathy* had a broken plank high up in the bow, way above the water line. That was it. I was lucky.

—David Bryce

friends and long-time customers, often former Widji counselors and Charlie's guides. Great grandchildren have been springing up rapidly, and if each is going to receive a Seliga canoe, it will represent a lot of work.

Remarkable Strength from Cherished Memories
On the blackest day of Joe's life, October 28, 2000, Nora passed away, closing a loving partnership that had endured more than 68 years. She had not been well in the months leading up to the autumn and, although Joe had not been feeling well himself, he dropped everything to care for her, making it possible for her to stay at their home despite her illness. Family members, especially daughter Nancy Richards, who lives in town, helped out each day, but Joe was at Nora's side every hour for weeks, until less than two days before her death she had to be admitted to the hospital. When she quietly took her last breath Joe was at her bedside.

Joe finds remarkable the strength he draws from the thousands of cherished memories of Nora that are etched vividly into his memory. The two kids in love, ignoring dozens of sound reasons why they weren't ready for marriage, had enough love and faith to pursue a life together and never look back.

After Nora passed away, Joe did not expect to build any more canoes. Although he was hospitalized twice with pneumonia, he slowly recovered and regained lost weight. Daughters Nancy Richards and JoAnn Nilsen jumped in to help. "Their mother would be very proud of them," Joe says with obvious pride and love. "They really brought me around." Laughingly he adds, "JoAnn joked, 'Don't expect me to cut up your meat.'"

The loving care was successful. When a MRI revealed that his lungs had cleared up, Joe started thinking about the unfinished canoe in the shop—the last canoe Nora had helped him with. "When I started working on the last canoe that Nora and I had bent ribs together on," Joe explains, "my intentions were to keep it for myself." But the master canoe builder who had not owned a canoe for half a century would have to wait a while longer. Rather than keeping the last canoe he and Nora had worked on together, Joe decided to donate it to Camp Widjiwagan.

Just as he had lain awake deliberating the best methods for repairing the Morris and building his form, Joe took care to craft what he felt would be the most appropriate lines to accompany the dedication. "It took me about a week and a half before I figured out what I wanted to say," he says. "Every time I would think of something, I ran to my tablet to write it down." Each word was carefully chosen:

After 60 years of helping me build the Seliga wood canvas canoes, I would like to present the last canoe Nora helped me with to

Joe's daughter Nancy Richards in 1990 in the canoe her father built for her more than two decades earlier. *Joe Seliga Collection*

**Camp Widjiwagan in memory of her:
Eleanor "Nora" Seliga, October 18, 1911–October 28, 2000.**

In return, the Widji staff presented Joe with a bronze sculpture modeled after a picture Ely newspaperman and artist "Jackpine" Bob Cary took of Joe with one of his canoes in the late 1960s.

Lifetime of Satisfying Accomplishments

Of Joe's 12 siblings, 4 are still living as of this writing: Ann, 95; Margaret, 86; Rudy, 77; and Ethel, 73. Joe lost two siblings, John and Helen, in 2000, at about the same time Nora died.

Joe's son Richard retired from banking and lives in Eveleth, Minnesota, less than an hour from Ely, with his wife, Nancy. Their son and daughter are grown with families of their own.

Daughter JoAnn Nilsen and husband Jan, who gave Joe and Nora three granddaughters and two grandsons, also adults, live just outside the Twin Cities in Cottage Grove, where JoAnn runs a day-care center. Jan is recently retired from the retailing business. Daughter Nancy, a homemaker, and her husband Tim, who drives a rig for a logging contractor, live nearby in Ely, and Nancy stops by her father's place every day. At last count, Joe had 16 great-grandchildren and feels blessed to have such a great family, with a growing fourth generation of happy and healthy kids. So far, no family member has indicated an interest in taking over Joe's celebrated canoe business.

Joe enjoys having lunch or dinner with friends at Brit's on Chapman Street or Vertin's on Sheridan. Friends are always stopping by, and he's constantly brewing coffee. He's a welcome guest and familiar fixture at Widjiwagan, where the staff know and love him, the young campers regard him with a sense of awe, and everyone enjoys his stories.

There are now 45 Seliga canoes at Widjiwagan, the first purchased in 1948. Most are still in service, and many have been used on the arduous "Voyageur" trips that have taken veteran campers far north into the barren lands. Just as the staff and campers have come to know and love Joe, these canoes have the respect, gratitude, and love of the hundreds of campers and counselors who have depended upon them.

It is in the woods at Widjiwagan, with sunlight filtering through the boughs of tall pines and bright, blue water dancing off the point, changing to green then to gold as it washes against the shore, that Joe has a chance to reflect on a lifetime of satisfying accomplishments and friendly faces. Often he says, "The best part about it all is the wonderful people I have met." He remembers the old Ely with a quiet wistfulness and sees Stephen and Anna loading picnic baskets into the canoes at the little boathouse on Shagawa, like a grainy clip from an old movie.

He looks back with satisfaction at a life's work that has come to be appreciated wherever canoes and craftsmanship

The husband-and-wife team pose for a photograph in June 1999 in the backyard of fellow Ely canoe builder Jeanne Bourquin.

are important. He remembers past fishing trips for walleyes, one when a major snowstorm made it difficult just to get back home. He recalls the broken Morris canoe fetched up in the spring torrent, caught against a fallen tree. "To this day, I don't know whether it was fallen by a beaver or the current," he says. But mostly now he sees images of Nora, as a beautiful young woman in love, a caring mother, a partner across the form from him, bending the steaming cedar, and, of course, in her kitchen serving her famous treats to old friends sitting around the table.

Joe Seliga has countless memories and accomplishments to cherish in his full life so far. Perhaps they are best reprised by a specification sheet that was printed in 1946, which states the code by which he has built his reputation and continues to live his life. At the bottom of the sheet it reads:

"There is only one quality in these canoes – THE BEST."

chapter four

Camp Widjiwagan and the Seliga Legacy

Joe at Camp Widjiwagan with the last canoe he and Nora built together. "Nora's canoe," which Joe presented to the camp in August 2001, is displayed there prominently and will be used only for special occasions.

As the late-summer sun slips from behind a towering thunderhead above the spruce-rimmed lake deep in Ontario's Quetico Provincial Park, the surface of the water explodes into a montage of tossing whitecaps and sparkling light, stippled by the sky's cerulean reflection. Along the protected shore of a ragged island, paddles flash as a pair of gray canoes make their way toward an inviting cove with a gravel beach arching between two tongues of deeply fissured granite. As the canoes draw nearer, three paddlers are discernable in each craft. The canoes move ahead on a course so straight, it seems there must be rails beneath the waves. Only the arresting yodel of a mother loon shepherding two half-grown chicks having a bad hair day causes the canoes to swerve from their target; now they veer away from the distressed loon family, affording them a wider berth. The loons settle down and the chicks resume pestering their harried protector for fresh fish.

Just when it appears that the swift canoes will be rammed well up onto the gravel, the bow men—or, in this case, bow girls—leap into the golden shallows, suddenly stopping the canoes before their keels brush even a single cobble. Soon, a bucket brigade is passing camping gear up from the floating canoes to the forest floor shaded beneath jackpines. As the duffle melts from their interiors, the canoes reveal the golden glow of the arching cedar ribs and varnished planking within. These are no ordinary canoes made of molded plastic or polyester-saturated fiberglass. These are wood-and-canvas veterans, and the perfectly sweeping gunwale lines and proud manner in which they dismiss the choppy waves indicate that they come with a pedigree, distinguished even within this demanding fraternity.

The canoes are Seligas, meticulously crafted in a workshop in Ely, Minnesota, by a builder with unparalleled experience and integrity.

The paddlers are campers and a counselor from Widjiwagan on Burntside Lake, a canoeing camp with a tradition of respect for the wilderness, fellow travelers, wildlife, and the canoes themselves. When the canoes are empty, two campers standing ankle deep in the lake lift each craft from the water and carry it to a resting spot thickly carpeted with pine needles and protected from hostile winds.

It's not surprising that the Seliga canoe legacy will continue long after Joe retires from canoe building. And it was probably inevitable that the core of Joe and Nora's work will be documented, celebrated, and continued on the grounds of Camp Widjiwagan, amid the surrounding natural beauty and the activity of young people busy shaping their lives. This is not because Widjiwagan acquired the greatest number of Seliga canoes over the years, but rather because the mission of "Widji,"

The bronze statue presented to Joe by Camp Widjiwagan in August 2001. The sculpture is based on the "Jackpine" Bob Cary photograph that was taken in the 1970s and appears on page 51.

as it is often called, has always meshed with the inherent qualities of a Seliga canoe: both embody strength through integrity and respect for the environment, and foster lasting enjoyment.

It was Widji counselor and Seliga friend Bob Binger who purchased Joe's first 18-foot "Voyager" off the new form in 1946. Widjiwagan became the first of many camps to purchase canoes from Joe when four 16-footers were delivered in 1948. And although several other camps acquired larger numbers of Seliga canoes through the 1950s and 1960s, it was Widjiwagan that continued purchasing and using Seligas through the 1990s and, incredibly, into the new millennium.

The Widji Story

The Widjiwagan experience got its start in June 1929 when the St. Paul YMCA paid $7,000 and took title to 74 acres of logged land along a point on Burntside Lake's northern arm. The selection and purchase of the property capped several years of planning, exploration, and negotiating by a small and dedicated group of individuals from the Twin Cities led by St. Paul businessman Julian Kirby. Because of raging hay fever, Kirby had spent many summers in the border lakes region upon the advice of his doctor. These enjoyable expeditions and the lessons he learned traveling through the wilderness by canoe were experiences he wanted to share with youngsters who might never have the chance to experience them on their own. A spiritual man, Kirby had supported the philosophies and programs of the YMCA for some time and believed that a special bond developed within a group of individuals traveling rigorously and wisely through the wilderness, and that this led to integrity and personal responsibility.

He expressed this conviction on a piece of birch bark, now hanging in Kirby Lodge, the camp's log dining hall:

Widjiwagan is the Ojibway Indian's word for "comradeship." We find it easy here to cultivate comradeship with our creator, comradeship with other fellows, and comradeship with the best fellow that each of us knows how to be.

Although Widjiwagan for a time implemented typical "resort" activities such as athletics, crafts, and horseback riding, canoe-tripping was an important activity from the outset, thanks to the efforts of the Widji's first caretaker, Wilbur Jeffery, who initiated formal canoe training in 1931. Three-day training sessions soon expanded into the six-day "milk run," beginning at the Moose River off the Echo Trail and ending back at Widjiwagan. In 1937, Bob Binger worked out the 14-day "Hunter's Island Trip" into the Quetico wilderness, which remained the standard trip for experienced campers for several years. Sessions for girls from nearby Camp Sherwood were implemented in 1937, but 10 years would pass before the first women's residency program was established.

Widjiwagan's tripping style was cast in stone in 1950 when, under the directorship of Armin "Whitey" Luehrs, the camp set the number of participants in a standard group at six—five campers and one counselor using two canoes. This ratio ensures reliable supervision, as well as maximum learning opportunities for the youngsters.

In 1955, Camp Widji developed the Voyageur program. Initially, Voyageur trips followed the routes of great Canadian wilderness explorers like Alexander Mackenzie. The young Voyageurs readily absorbed the fascinating history of the Canadian north, and Ely resident and environmentalist Sigurd Olson was consulted in the program's development. A trip might begin at Grand Portage on Lake Superior and end more than 1,000 miles later at the Arctic Ocean after traversing northwestern Canada's barren lands. Since such trips took many months or even years to negotiate, the long routes were divided into segments that succeeding Widji trips could cover in five weeks each year until the entire route was accomplished. Naturally, Voyageur trips were open to only the

Two Camp Widjiwagan counselors demonstrate the proper way to take a Seliga canoe—or, as Joe would say, *any* canoe—out of the water.

most experienced campers, and because billets were limited, participants were carefully screened and selected before invitations were extended. To be invited as a Voyageur became a source of justified pride for any serious Widji camper. In 1956, just a year after the program was implemented, the first women's Voyageur trip was floated, retracing the boys' route of the previous season.

Widjiwagan Today

Widjiwagan today is a thriving, multifaceted institution offering year-round programs for both boys and girls, as well as adults, schools, and families. Still grounded in the traditions and ideals of Julian Kirby, Widji's mission remains the same: "To build in young people, respect for self, the community, and the environment, through wilderness adventure and environmental education."

Fourteen full-time staff members are led by Executive Director Tom Kranz, who lives onsite with his family during the regular season and travels back and forth between Widji and his home near the Twin Cities the rest of the year. In the year 2000, more than 2,000 people participated in the camps' various programs. Approximately 700 of that total were summer campers, 85 percent of them in the canoe-tripping program, which is organized into various categories: 10-day introductory trips for first-year campers, 14-day BWCAW trips, 17-day Quetico trips, and 27-day Explorer and advanced Explorer trips. Widjiwagan sent out seven Voyageur trips to destinations like the Dubawnt and Back Rivers, as well as four "Mountaineer" groups on 36- to 39-day hikes in the Arctic National Wildlife Refuge and the Kluane National Park Reserve.

Onsite, Tom Kranz looks relaxed if not actually disheveled. Ruggedly built, the former college football player has a boyish grin and an easygoing manner, and is apparently at ease with the responsibility of guiding the major endeavor Widjiwagan has become. Off the top of his head, he accurately rattles off financial figures, enrollments, dates, and projections. He also has a good rapport with staff and counselors encountered along Widji's byways shaded beneath the camp's tall pines. Many of them were planted by Wilbur Jeffery, Widji's first caretaker, and most survived the great blow of July 4, 1999, that leveled millions of trees in the BWCAW.

Kranz himself was a Widji camper in the late 1960s, and has been familiar with the traditions, programs, and the special spirit of Widjiwagan most of his life. He arrived at his position from a similar responsibility at another YMCA camp in the area—Camp DuNord—that specializes in one-week camp programs for families.

A Seliga canoe is presented to outgoing Widji director Bob Rick (left) in 1989. Camp manager Joe Smith is to the right of Joe and Nora.
Joe Seliga Collection

Kranz depends daily on the industry and resourcefulness of his property manager, Joe Smith, another square-jawed former Widji Voyageur and counselor. Joe spent time during and after college in Missoula, Montana, tracking and tagging wolves and grizzly bears with renowned biologist David Mech, whose work with the animals is well known among colleagues nationwide, and who was instrumental in developing Ely's International Wolf Center. Smith also spent a number of years as an independent logger out of Grand Marais, Minnesota, before returning to Widji in 1984 with his wife Lindsey and family.

Just down a shady path, an imposing log structure built in an "L" configuration greets visitors with wide porches facing a thin band of trees and Burntside Lake sparkling just beyond. Like Kirby Lodge, the building is a traditional log construction on a massive scale, with tightly fit notches, chisel-pointed ends at the corners, and logs of impressive length and girth. One leg of the "L" is used for "packing out" or provisioning the various trips, and the other is the canoe shop itself. The facility represents a priority of Kranz's predecessor, Rolfe Thompson, come to completion.

Current camp director Tom Kranz (left) and Widjiwagan manager Joe Smith (right), with Joe and one of Seliga's 16-footers.

Widji campers and counselors assess available jobs inside the camp's spacious log canoe shop.

Inside are 2,000 square feet of uninterrupted, brightly lit space that is well on its way to being fitted out as a well-equipped canoe shop with a measure of northwoods ambiance. Three counselors currently between trips are making paddles, each different and each reflecting the maker's ideas as to what constitutes a good blade.

A young man bent over a damaged Seliga canoe shed of its canvas, clinches the tacks that hold a replacement rib in place. A windstorm dropped a tree on the canoe and the affected quarter needs new ribs and planking. The young craftsman is Michael Prezioso, the full-time canoe master at Widji whose job it is to maintain and upgrade the camp's fleet of over 100 wooden canoes, some of which have served Widji since the 1930s.

Smith explains that, until recently, the repairs were often piecemeal and hurried—band- aids, really—just to get the canoes seaworthy for the season, or even just the next trip. Occasionally, a lucky canoe would be sent to Joe's or another builder's shop for major rehab work, but the canoes in need

Using one of the camp's 45 Seliga canoes, Widji counselors teach a group of campers the fundamentals of wooden canoe construction.

of real attention quickly began to outnumber those being restored. With Prezioso, who has taken courses in canoe building and restoration, working full time and actually training interested staff members, it is anticipated that 7 to 12 canoes can be rehabilitated—including new canvas—each year.

Kranz points out that some of the less-serious projects can be tackled under Michael's supervision during fall and winter education sessions billed as winter canoe workshops. The programs are open to adults as well as kids, and include programs for youngsters in group homes and home placement situations.

The Seliga Endowment and "Nora's Canoe"

The Nora and Joe Seliga Wood Canoe Endowment was launched with the building of the new canoe shop in 1998. At that time, it was determined that for Widjiwagan to rehabilitate and maintain its existing fleet and add a few new wooden canoes each year would require an endowment of nearly $1 million. Because of Seliga's close ties to Widjiwagan, Joe had already determined that the camp would be the ideal permanent home for his forms and the appropriate guardian of the Seliga canoe legacy.

The idea sat well with the directors and alumni, and the campaign was launched with an incredibly generous gift of $250,000 from a single donor. Other major contributions followed, until the fund stood at $490,000 in 2001, almost halfway to its ultimate goal. It is a testament to the importance of Seliga canoes in the lives of former counselors and campers, as well as an honor to Joe that is likely unparalleled in his field.

The goal of the wooden canoe program at Widjiwagan is not to build and sell Seliga canoes once Joe turns over his form. Rather, it is one more way to instill respect and integrity in those who become involved, and to provide an exciting new focus for future environmental education programs. At the same time, Widji's fleet of wooden canoes will grow and the canoes that have served so well for so long will be maintained in the manner they deserve.

On August 25, 2001, at a well-attended ceremony, Joe presented Camp Widjiwagan with the last canoe he and Nora built together. The gesture and accompanying statement from Joe spoke volumes on love, partnership, and commitment. It also simultaneously bestowed a special honor and conferred a

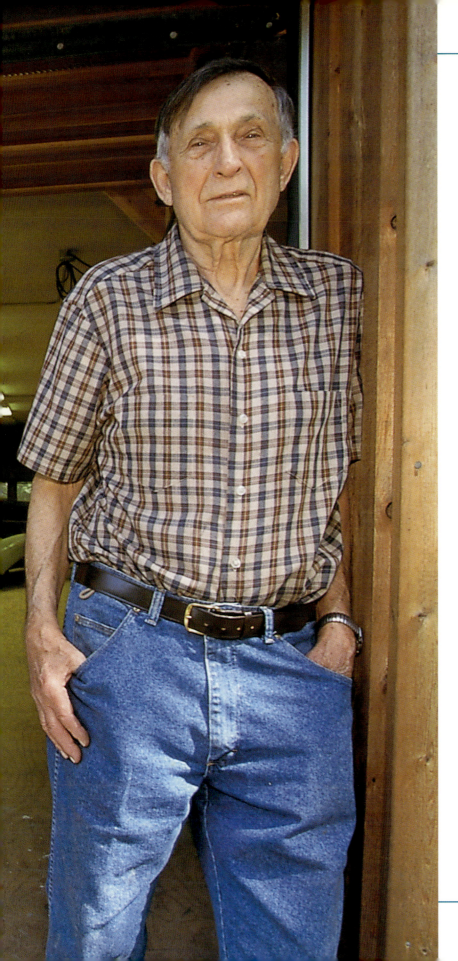

serious responsibility on Widjiwagan. On behalf of past, present, and future Widji staff and campers, Kranz expressed how much the Seliga canoes have contributed to the "Widji Way," and promised that the spirit and integrity of Seliga canoes would continue to play a major role in the camp's mission.

They were not idle promises. "Nora's canoe" will not be put in general service, but will be displayed prominently on supports and perhaps put in the water for special events. In the meantime, back at the log canoe shop, Prezioso restores decades-old Seliga canoes in need of help and teaches young counselors the intricacies of the craft. Joe's old square-stern form is in the shop, along with the 15-foot Morris and its modifications as a building form. The healthy endowment ensures that the work will be continued and that paddling and caring for a Seliga canoe will remain as important to future Widji campers as it has been to those of the past and present.

Joe stands in the doorway of the Widjiwagan canoe shop that will continue his legacy. Currently, the building is home to Joe's old square-stern form and the 15-foot B. N. Morris that he adapted as a form in 1937.

chapter five

Building the Seliga Canoe

Joe displays a handsome new canoe outside the modest shop that has served him for half a century. A finished Seliga canoe embodies all the grace and character that only 65 years of experience can impart.

Preparing Stock

Quality materials play a key role in the beauty and longevity of any good wood-and-canvas canoe, and they have almost always been scarce. Joe Seliga has made it a career-long quest to find and obtain the best materials available in the greater Midwest, if not locally. When local and regional materials prove unsuitable or impossible to find, Joe turns to lumber from the West Coast.

Only one species of wood—northern white cedar—has just the right balance of weight, color, strength, and flexibility to make the transverse frames, called ribs, for a canoe. Since ribs are not especially long—less than 5 feet—Joe has never encountered great difficulty in locating his rib stock locally, or at least regionally. Long, "clear" planking stock, however, is another matter. White cedars typically do not grow as tall as other softwoods and are often thick, with branches the length of their trunks. Whenever white cedar that is free of knots is available in sufficient lengths for planking (planking stock need not run the full length of the canoe), Joe uses it. He especially values cedar with a close vertical grain just beneath the bark. Oddly enough, Joe currently has some of the finest white cedar he has seen in his long building career.

"After a board meeting at Sommers in September, some directors came over to the shop and told me a big cedar tree had fallen over at the camp," Joe explains. "The butt log was 16 feet long, clear, and over 2 feet in diameter, and they asked me if I wanted it. 'Oh boy, you bet I do,' I told them. Tim [Richards, Joe's son-in-law] trucked it to the mill, and you should see the lumber. I've waited 65 years to find planking stock like this so close to home."

Whenever native planking stock is not available, western red cedar is Joe's favorite substitute. During the 1950s and 1960s, Joe had purchased long, 6-inch-wide lengths of vertical-grained cedar from a Twin Cities supplier. Because of the lumber's width, which was too wide for Joe to re-saw, he had the dealer re-saw it to 1/4-inch thickness and then planed it to 5/32 inch in his shop.

Sitka spruce, another western species, is Joe's choice for the full-length inner gunwales (inwales), while Honduras mahogany from Twin Cities suppliers is normally used for outer gunwales. Black ash—white ash is not common in the north country—works best for the stems and thwarts. It is tough, yet flexible, which is important for stem stock, and it bends readily after steaming or boiling.

Joe most often uses a closed-grained hardwood like black cherry for the decks, although ash and mahogany are suitable despite their more-open grains.

(above) Joe finds that boiling the cedar ribs and ash stems is more effective than steaming. This homemade aluminum tank with a sliding top at each end works well for him. The burner beneath is fired by propane gas. The tank works equally well for pre-soaking wood to be bent

(right) Joe cuts the white cedar rib blanks to 2-1/4 inches wide and 3/8 inch thick, then reduces them to a thickness of 5/16 inch with his thickness planer. He prepares about 60 at a time for a single canoe.

(opposite) After cutting the rib blanks to approximate lengths, Joe uses a sliding jig to taper both sides of the stock, making the ribs narrower at the top for a finer appearance inside the canoe. Joe saves every useful scrap; those that can't be used in the building process help fuel the shop's wood stove.

(above left) Joe uses an inverted router mounted beneath a smooth surface and a rounding-over bit to shape the edges of the ribs.

(above right) The completed ribs are sanded before they are placed in the boiler, even though they will need sanding again once inside the canoe.

(above) The canoe's ash stems must be pre-bent on a separate jig several days before beginning a canoe. Here, Joe uses pliers as tongs to remove the hot stem stock from the boiling water.

(right) A galvanized steel compression strap helps prevent the grain on the outside surface of the stem stock from stretching excessively and failing. Joe takes his time as he pulls the stem around the jig.

(above) Joe has a C-clamp handy to fasten the 7/8-inch-thick stem stock in place as he completes the bend.

(right) Normally, Joe bends stock wide enough for a pair of stems, but he doesn't waste narrower stock if it's suitable. Having bent his available stock, Joe keeps them on the jig until needed, allowing them to set in the proper configuration.

(left) Before slicing the wide stem stock into a pair of stems on the table saw, Joe marks the notches on the bottom face of the stem where the ribs will cross.

(below) Joe uses a dado head on his table saw to cut the notches for the ribs.

(right) Joe uses the same dado head tilted at an angle to cut a bevel where the planking will meet the curved portion of the stem.

(below) Joe inspects a completed stem, with its smooth, beveled curve and notches to accommodate the ribs.

(above left) The beveled portion of the stem ends just before reaching the first notch. The lip running along the top surface of the bevel is removed on the band saw.

(above right) Joe stamps his serial numbers onto the flat of each stem. Number 97 614 7, for example indicates canoe number 614, built in July (seventh month) 1997.

(right) Joe uses a separate jig to taper the ends of the inwales. This results in a finer appearance at the decks.

Setting up the Form

A solidly built form representing the exact shape of the inside of the finished canoe was the key component that enabled manufacturers to build any number of identical wooden canoes in an efficient, production-line manner. The first canoe form was developed around 1880 in Bangor, Maine, by a woodsman-turned-boat-builder named E. H Gerrish.

Joe Seliga's form was built in 1946 to produce 18-foot canoes that were modifications of the B. N. Morris canoe that played such an important role in his youth. The romanticized lines of the Morris were extravagantly graceful, and sweet to look at, but less than practical for use in wilderness canoe travel. Joe lowered the elegant bow by a couple of inches to a more reasonable height and swelled out the narrow entry a bit, allowing the canoe to better rise up on waves when loaded. Joe kept just enough tumblehome along the sides to retain a handsome appearance without inviting spray from wave tops to wash aboard. The result was a handsome, portageable and seaworthy craft that hinted of its Morris roots while addressing itself to the requirements of a working canoe. In the field, the 18-foot length proved awkward at tighter spots on border lakes portages, so in 1950 Joe reworked the ends of the form, shortening it to 17 feet.

Joe's form is built of spruce strips over solid molds spaced 18 inches (12 inches near the ends) and fitted with 16-gauge galvanized steel bands that dictate where to bend the ribs and automatically clinch the tacks as he fastens the planking. Because the shapes of the canoe's bow and stern are determined by the pre-bent stems and not by the form itself, Joe, like many other builders, did not incorporate the curved shapes into the form, instead ending the form at the last bendable rib.

Slots at each end accommodate the straight, notched portions of the stems, as well as a recessed backup strip on each side to locate the inwales. The form, weighing close to 300 pounds, is clamped to a pair of wheeled dollies that enable Joe to move it around as necessary.

The two inwales that Joe tapered on his table saw are taped together and their ends boiled for about an hour before Joe bends them around a long jig to introduce a little curve into their ends to match the rise of the sheer. Notice they're being bent on a canoe that's already planked; in Joe's shop, there are always canoes in different states of construction.

(above) The bent inwales are kept on the jig at least overnight and often for several days. Here, Joe removes the tape that binds the pair of inwales together.

(right) Joe's form, which is the same shape as the inside of a canoe, has stood the test of time and hundreds of canoes. The ribs are bent over the metal bands, and when the planks are fastened to them, the sharp, pointed brass tacks clinch tightly upon striking the 16-gauge galvanized steel.

(top opposite) One of the notched stems rests in its slot on the form. The plastic wrap will prevent the metal bands from staining the hot, wet ribs.

(left opposite) Joe uses a bit brace to fasten the metal tabs that hold one of the pre-bent inwales in its channel.

(above) Joe works the end of the inwale into position. The thousands of splatters dotting the floor of Joe's workshop represent every color he has ever painted his canoes. Remarkably, many of them survived the 1994 fire that nearly took the shop.

(above) A strongback bolted to one side of the centerline will tightly hold the boiled ribs to the form.

(left) Joe takes a minute to record the serial number of the canoe being built.

Bending Ribs

There is always an air of excitement when hot, steaming ribs are pulled from the boiling tank, slid beneath the strongback, and wrapped around the form. The pliability of the boiled ribs seems somehow magical, beyond belief.

The idea of lightweight bent ribs as framing was developed independently in both the New and Old Worlds. In Europe, although large vessels were framed with huge ribs sawn to shape from timbers, the frames of small craft were frequently steamed or boiled and installed while still hot into the overlapped (hence, lapstrake) planks of the boats. Native American bark-canoe builders poured hot water over green ribs and, pinning them to the ground, bent them around the knee and stacked them in bundles. Later, the pre-bent ribs were inserted one at a time inside the pre-shaped heavy bark skin.

It was not until the development of the solid canoe form in the 1880s that it became practical to bend the ribs over the shape before the planking was fitted. Joe Seliga has used both steaming and boiling as techniques to soften flat cedar ribs. Each method has it advantages, but Joe finds that boiling prevents the ribs from drying out and becoming brittle, as they sometimes do if kept too long in the steam box. In addition, Joe is vigilant about changing the water in his boiler, because dust and oils in the cedar soon dirty the water to the point where it stains the light-colored wood.

For decades, bending ribs was a chore shared with Nora. It is a natural process for two people—one on each side of the canoe, holding the hot rib flat to the form near the strongback, stretching it around, and nailing its end to the inwale. With Nora gone, though, Joe chooses to build his canoes alone rather than seeking a helper, even though there are dozens of friends who would be pleased to lend a hand. Instead, Joe has developed ways to do it alone, using props, clamps, and the ingenuity that got him started in the first place. Also, although he has figured out how to accomplish the rib-bending without his partner, each time he does, he forgets for a moment that Nora is not at the other end.

One of Joe's favorite hammers has an angled handle he fashioned himself to provide better contact in tight spots.

(above) Joe pulls a boiled rib out of the tank. Like many craftsmen, Joe has developed the habit of keeping nails handy in his mouth.

(left) The softened ribs bend easily around the form, and each end is fastened to the inwale with a single galvanized nail. At the point where the strongback ends, Joe holds the rib tightly to the form with a wedge propped from above. When Nora was alive helping Joe, this was unnecessary

The first step of bending a rib solo is to slide the hot frame under the strongback.

(above) Joe bends and fastens one end of a rib. Notice the wide wooden wedges between the strongback and the already bent ribs to keep them tight to the form.

(right) Joe walks around or sometimes crawls under the canoe to bend and fasten the other end. Notice that the ribs are made extra long–Joe will trim them later.

In Joe's modest-sized shop, the form is never far from the boiler. Once taken from the box, the ribs remain pliable for a full minute or two, giving Joe enough time, so he needn't hurry—but he can't waste time, either.

(left opposite) Near the ends of the form, Joe can reach over to bend both ends of the rib, then nail them one side at a time.

(left) At the bow and stern of the canoe, where the bend is too severe to bend a rib, two "cant" ribs are prepared by beveling and then nailing them to the stem, bending them…

(above) …nailing them to the inwales, and further securing them with a C-clamp until they are dry. The cant ribs will be removed and set aside while the canoe is planked and reinstalled when the hull is off the form. Notice the notched wooden block that temporarily holds the inwales together at the stem.

(left) Eventually, Joe gets to the final rib and the canoe's skeleton is about complete.

(below) While the ribs are still "green," Joe bolts two additional strongbacks alongside the one at center to hold the ribs flat to the form while they dry.

(below) By the following day, the ribs have dried into shape. Joe uses a long board with an aggressive sandpaper surface to sand across the backs of the ribs and ensure their fairness to one another. With the skillfully bent ribs and Joe's nearly perfect form (it would be impossible to make a perfect form), little effort is needed to bring the ribs into line.

(right) To facilitate fairing the bottom of the canoe, Joe removes the extra strongbacks.

Planking

One feature that makes it possible to build the hull of a wood-and-canvas canoe over a form relatively quickly is the thin dimension and flexibility of the longitudinal planking.

Since the waterproof integrity of the canoe is ensured by the treated canvas covering and not by the actual joints along each planking seam, the material can remain thin, resulting in a canoe generally light enough to portage. Because planking is only 5/32-inch thick, the cedar must be of good quality and largely free of knots. Of the two varieties commonly used in planking, northern white is considered more flexible than western red. The western cedar, however, is often easier to obtain in long, clear lengths, and its rich color can create a handsome contrast against the lighter-hued ribs.

All the planks or "strakes" in a canoe need not be full length, but the fewer butt joints on the ribs in a canoe, the better in terms of overall hull strength. Like many builders, Joe normally works with planking stock that ranges from 8 to 12 feet in length. The flexibility of this thin stock allows the builder to twist and bend it to some degree, especially after soaking it in hot water. This means that the first four or five planks along the bottom on either side of the centerline can be attached with relatively little shaping and fitting. Because shapes need not be cut from extra-wide planks, thereby creating considerable waste, this saves time and material.

Eventually, though, the builder must address the fact that the canoe is a complex shape and that its variable girth and the complexities of the curves at the turn of its bilge make it necessary to determine and cut tapers, shapes, and "gores" to make the planks fit. These shapes are distinct on each model of canoe to fill in this space efficiently and aesthetically—and no one is more familiar with a planking pattern than Seliga is with his 17-foot design. Working steadily, Joe figures he can plank an entire canoe in 8 to 10 hours. "But who gets to work steady without interruptions for that long?" he jokes.

Re-sawing the 1-inch-thick stock into 1/4-inch planks also makes good sense economically, and Joe, who is never one to waste material, appreciates that.

Joe re-saws all his planking on his trusty 70-year-old Sears table saw, setting the fence for a 1/4-inch cut, standing the 1-inch stock on its edge against the fence, and pushing the whole length of plank past the blade. Since his blade will cut only 2 inches of material at a pass and his planking averages 3 inches wide, he must turn the stock over and send it through a second time to finish the cut. He then splits the remaining 5/8-inch stock with two additional passes, thus ending up with three 1/4-inch-thick planks that are 3 inches wide and however long. There are over 300 linear feet of planking in one of his canoes, which represents quite an investment in work.

Once re-sawn, the 1/4-inch planks must be planed to 5/32 inch and sanded smooth on one side. They are fastened to the ribs with 11/16-inch brass canoe tacks whose extremely sharp tips clinch when they strike the metal bands of the form. The heads of the tacks are slightly rounded.

(opposite left) Joe uses a palm sander to smooth one side of the planed planks. Since the ribs make it impossible to do a good job inside the canoe, this is the only opportunity to get the job done.

(left) The planking must be soaked with hot water, wherever the wood will be expected to bend or twist, particularly along the turn of the bilge.

(above) The first two planks, sometimes called "strakes," along the centerline are called garboards and must be twisted down at the ends in order to run past the stems. The garboards require repeated applications of hot water to make them twist without cracking. Along the straight portion of the stem beneath, the planking is nailed with galvanized nails. Here, Joe shapes the garboard with his block plane after wetting it and bending its end around.

(right) Once bent and trimmed, Joe finishes fastening the garboards with more tiny galvanized nails.

(above) Little shaping is required of the planks running along the inverted bottom. What little is needed at the ends can be done with a block plane after they're in place.

(right) Joe's nailing pattern is four tacks to each rib placed in an alternating pattern and continued on adjacent strakes. Joe is careful not to make the pattern too wide and risk the tacks splitting the edges of the ribs on the inside.

(top opposite) Joe sights down a plank for any natural curve he might be able to use while shaping the planks for the turn of the bilge.

(bottom opposite) One leaf of Joe's homemade steel goring gauge slides beneath a plank in need of shaping, which is temporarily attached with a nylon strap. A lip at the end contacts the edge of the plank beneath. The upper leaf is of equal length and indicates how much will have to be taken off the new plank. Joe gets a reading at each rib and by connecting the marks he gets the shape of the tapered or "gored" plank.

(left) With the taper marked, Joe removes the plank and takes it to the table saw, where he can rough cut the shape.

(left) He will use his block plane to make the final fit of the planking. The spoke shave is better for shaping curved pieces held in a vice.

(below) Joe straps the shaped plank back into position and begins tacking it on.

(left) Around the tight turn of the bilge, every plank requires soaking with hot water from the boiler.

(lower left) When the two gored planks that make up for the reduced girth of the canoe are not long enough to run out naturally, Joe determines the shape of a single wedged-shaped piece that will cover the last couple of feet.

(left) Joe shapes the wedge-shaped piece by eye, on the spot.

(bottom) The piece is nailed in place.

(left) Once the tapered wedge is in place, Joe adds a narrow plank that runs all the way to the stem.

(bottom) The finished planking job. The remaining "sheer" plank must be fit when the canoe is off the form, otherwise it would be impossible to release the tabs that hold the inwale onto the form. The planking is not yet nailed to the stem for the same reason.

Completing the Hull

Pulling the canoe off the form is like assisting at a birth or witnessing a metamorphosis. The light, flexible, and almost ethereal shell is liberated from the dark, heavy form, and although it mirrors the form's shape, its essence is entirely different—more graceful and fragile, and somehow free.

Completing the hull seems like a big step, but is really only the beginning of another phase of construction that involves many smaller steps. Coaxing the hull into its proper shape, ensuring the plumbness of the stems, and closing up the ends requires the trained eye Joe has developed through his years of experience.

Although Seliga's canoes are built over the same form and are on the surface identical in length, beam (width), depth, and overall shape, each will have its own personality. Because wood is the principle material in the canoe, each one will display a unique blend of grain, color, marbling of light sapwood and darker heartwood, and even signature blemishes such as a harmless, tiny knot up near an end. Canoes are especially subject to this when you consider the sheer number of individual pieces: four gunwales (two spruce inwales and two mahogany outer gunwales or "rails"); two decks of hardwood, perhaps different varieties from canoe to canoe; 50 individual ribs; perhaps 30 sections of planking, depending upon length; two bent stems; two thwarts and a portaging yoke; and two caned seats, each made of four ash pieces. The variety of combinations is perhaps why builders like Joe never tire of watching their canoes develop, no matter how many years they're in the business.

If he wanted to, Joe could easily change minor characteristics of the canoe at this stage, and he has been known to do so for special orders. He could, for example, pull the inwales in closer together, adding to the tumblehome and slightly increasing the gentle arch across the bottom of the canoe. He could lift the inwales an inch higher at the ends to more closely resemble the Morris, or put in wider decks to eliminate the reverse curve noticeable there. He has this final chance to subtly change small aspects of the canoe before it is forever locked into place. But mostly he resists this temptation. Many years of experiment and development have gone into his design, and most customers expect—and get—the handsome model that's as close to the ideal as Joe can make it.

(opposite) After making sure all the planking tacks are well seated, Joe sponges on hot water, which will swell out any hammer "blossoms," or dents, that are evident in the soft cedar.

(top left) Joe temporarily stretches a plastic cover over the newly wetted hull, ensuring the wood will not dry out before the dents have had a chance to swell out.

(middle left) Once the cedar has dried, usually the next day, and with the hull still on the form, Joe uses a belt sander on the bottom of the outer hull, mostly to smooth the seams between the planks. In the days before the belt sander, Joe would do this by hand, using sandpaper on a long board. The step would take an hour or more, rather than the 15 or 20 minutes it does today.

(bottom left) After vacuuming, Joe brushes on a film of linseed oil that has been heated, but not to the boiling point, to seal the outside bottom of the hull.

With the hull ready to be freed from the form, Joe uses a brace to remove the metal retaining tabs. Notice the cardboard box on which he sets the tabs to protect the newly sanded surface of the hull.

(above) As the tabs are removed, the cedar ribs spring the loosened inwales from their slots. Working his way along the canoe, Joe lifts one end free, balances it on the form, and then frees the other end.

(right) The liberated hull perched on the form looks almost like a reflection. At this stage, with the plank ends still unfastened to the stems and no structural cross pieces, the hull is very flexible.

(left) Placing the hull on horses, Joe pulls it back to its approximate shape, using temporary cross spalls that straddle the inwales amidships and near each end. The natural outward tension of the bent ribs holds the crosspieces in place. Joe begins the critical joining of stem and inwales by bringing the inwales together and sawing between them. Among woodworkers, this is a common practice to achieve a fine fit between two pieces of wood.

(right) When he gets close, Joe determines the proper length, and thus the correct height, of the stem by measuring from the inside end with a batten. Excess length is lopped off and the stem sits just beneath the inwales, slightly supporting their ends.

(right) When Joe is satisfied with the joint, he clamps both inwales and the stem together using hardwood protectors.

(bottom) To ensure the stems are plumb, Joe first levels the canoe athwart ships. He has already trimmed the tops of the ribs close to the inwales with a handsaw.

(above) With the canoe level across, and an ancient spotlight illuminating the end, Joe visually lines the edge of the level alongside the stem and checks the bubble. If the stem is not perfectly plumb, he can still adjust its position by sawing a sliver off one of the inwales at the joint, which pulls the stem top slightly in that direction.

(right) Once satisfied, Joe locks the stem in place by driving a galvanized nail through the joint into the top of the stem. To prevent splitting, he pre-drills the hole for the nail.

(left) Joe marks and cuts off the excess planking running past the stem.

(right) Using his block plane, he fits the planks tightly to one another and fastens them to the stem with tiny galvanized nails. When nailing, he backs up the stem with a clinching iron to keep it from shifting.

(**above**) Joe then refits the cant ribs he removed before planking. They still have some of their set from drying on the form. He shapes and bevels the lower ends to fit between the stem and the garboard planks.

(**top right**) Joe cuts the rib to its exact length after test fitting it in the end of the canoe. Back at the table saw, he cuts a notch in the top that will fit perfectly at the inwale, resulting in a thin rib top that will later allow the outer gunwale to fit alongside.

(**right**) Joe holds his clinching iron along the inside of the cant rib while he hammers in tacks from the outside.

Installing Decks and Sanding the Hull

Nearly every canoe company, and just about every individual builder, uses a deck pattern that is identifiable and often personal. Certain manufacturers used similar shapes, yet subtle differences made them distinctive. On an Old Town canoe, the wide ends of the decks have a deep indentation cut out that is almost square across the inside, as opposed to arched. The "horns" on either side have little steps cut into them—two steps on older models, and just one on more recent canoes. Ely builder Jeanne Bourquin uses a similar configuration, only the indentation is deeper and the steps more pronounced. On early E. M. White canoes, the decks had two small arches cut out side by side like two bites out of a sandwich with a point in the middle. On other Whites, the decks have a wider single arch and the spruce decks on his capable but rough-and-ready guide models might be cut square across with no detailing, just a triangle.

E. H. Gerrish of Bangor, Maine, the first wood-and-canvas-canoe manufacturer, leaned toward heart-shaped decks and perhaps provided the inspiration for B. N. Morris, who used this shape almost exclusively and had a profound influence on many builders, including Joe Seliga. The Chestnut brothers of New Brunswick, Canada, were first impressed by the Morris canoes that wound up on the St. John River in Fredericton, having completed trips from northern Maine. Chestnut actively recruited builders from established Maine factories, which probably explains their adoption of the heart-shaped pattern. When celebrated New York builder J. H. Rushton was forced by market pressures to start building wood-and-canvas canoes (which he considered inferior to his all-wood canoes), another Mainer with Morris connections named Melvin Roundy was hired as his manager and brought the heart-shaped pattern with him.

After the 1920 fire at the B. N. Morris plant, another displaced Morris foreman was hired by the Kennebec Canoe Company of Waterville, Maine, and the heart shapes turned up on the Kennebec canoes as well. Contemporary Atkinson, Maine, builder Rollin Thurlow has been heavily influenced by White, Gerrish, and especially Morris, so it's no surprise that he uses his own unique version of the heart-shaped deck.

And so we come to Joe Seliga, who grew up in Morris canoes and considers Bert Morris to be his mentor. Naturally, Joe has his pleasing version of the popular pattern. Truly, the key word here is "version," because, although all the builders above use or used heart-shaped deck patterns, each is subtly different—an astute scholar of wooden canoes would never confuse a Morris deck with a Rushton, or a Thurlow with a Gerrish or a Joe Seliga. But its near universality is probably due to the fact that it is a naturally beautiful pattern, and as Joe simply states, "I like the heart-shaped deck pattern. To me they're the prettiest."

As for sanding, even a carefully built canoe can be made or broken by the quality and thoroughness of it. And just as a fine canoe can fail to reach its aesthetic potential if the sanding falls short, a poorly made canoe cannot be made right with even the most meticulous sanding. No one knows this better than Joe Seliga, and, while carefully building his canoes, he never fails to bring out all the sanding tools at his command and apply them seriously and efficiently.

The decks, sometimes called "breast hooks," must also be boiled and bent to reflect the canoe's upward sweep at the ends of the gunwales. This press, which is operated by tightening the large C-clamps, bends the upward sweep into the decks and also forms a small crown across the width of the pieces. Here, one deck has already been removed.

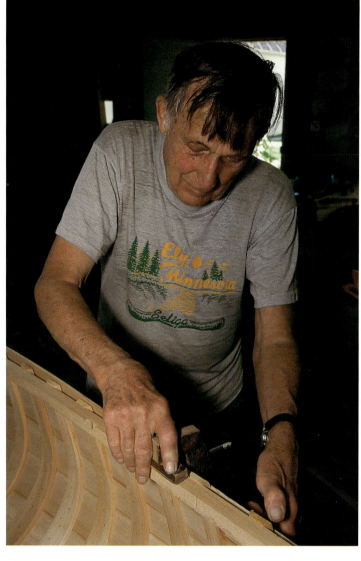

(top left opposite) Joe takes the second deck from the press. The decks have a blunt cutout at this stage to make them bend more easily in the press. While Joe sometimes uses ash or mahogany for his decks, the most suitable wood is closed-grain black cherry like that used here.

(bottom left opposite) Joe uses the band saw to cut the deep "V" in the heart-shaped deck. If he did this before boiling the deck, it would likely split right up the center.

(top right opposite) Holding the deck almost upright and working by hand, Joe removes a beveled slice of wood from the undersides of the shaped end, resulting in a more delicate appearance.

(bottom right opposite) The shaped deck is then placed in position and fastened with bronze screws. Later, when the outer gunwales are installed, Joe will shape a pleasing crown onto the deck's top surface using a sander.

(above left) Next, Joe cuts and fits the pieces of the sheer plank to complete the planking job. With no form to support the ribs or clinch the nails, he'll use a clinching iron on the inside of the rib. Note the bottom planks have already been oiled.

(above right) Joe runs a marking gauge with a pencil in it along the inwale. This provides an even guideline along the sheer plank, about 1/4 inch below the inwale, at which height it will be cut with a utility knife. Later, a lip on the outer gunwale will fit snuggly along this 1/4-inch slot, covering the raw edges of the sheer plank and canvas.

(above) Taking advantage of a breeze outside his shop, Joe begins sanding the ribs. He sands the long runs of the ribs along the bottom with a long-based orbital sander. Joe's use of a dust mask is sporadic. For intense sanding indoors, he'll sometimes wear a light-duty mask. With good ventilation or when working outdoors, his usage depends on the direction of the wind. Joe seems blessed with a constitution that is little affected by wood dust, just as it was more or less impervious to debris in the mines.

(right) The inside curves of the ribs are more easily sanded with a small palm sander.

There are always spots and edges that require some careful hand sanding.

(top left) Joe uses a disk sander on the crowned decks.

(left) Finally, Joe skillfully employs a belt sander to smooth the outside surface that hasn't already been sanded while the canoe was still on the form.

(top right) Joe signs the outside of each canoe before oiling and canvassing. Before Nora died, the inscription read, "Built by Nora and Joe Seliga," followed by the date. Today it reads, "Built by Joe Seliga," followed by the date and a statement that reveals Nora's continued importance in Joe's work: "Eleanor 'Nora' Seliga, October 18, 1911–October 28, 2000."

(left) After heating linseed oil in the electric frying pan, Joe applies it to the interior of the canoe, bringing out the rich tones and beautiful grains of the cedar. If time permits, he will apply a coat of spar varnish to the interior the following day, allowing it to dry overnight before canvassing.

(bottom) Joe oils the portion of the outer surface that was not previously treated.

Canvassing

Covering a complex shape like a canoe with a single piece of heavy, dry canvas and getting the skin uniformly taut without any bags or wrinkles can be a challenging exercise. To accomplish the task effectively, it is important to stretch the canvas around the hull while applying a considerable amount of tension to the whole length of material. The large canoe companies performed this task by stretching a folded length of canvas (slightly longer than the canoe itself) between a fixed anchor and a winch or come-along. The canoe was placed right side up in the enveloping fold, the tension increased, and enough weight or vertical pressure applied to balance the horizontal tension. The canvas was then trimmed close to the inwale and pulled around the hull at each rib with special pliers and fastened.

Because Joe has learned canoe building largely on his own, he does the actual stretching with the canoe upside down on horses. Joe has performed this task so often that he probably could do it in his sleep. He has also developed a unique trick to maintain the tension on the canvas even when it is released from the pulling mechanism, allowing him to turn the canoe right side up for final pulling and stapling along the gunwale.

Seliga uses Number 10 Midwest duck exclusively because it is tightly woven and extremely tough. The porous white cloth must be waterproofed and the weave filled with an abrasion-resistant yet flexible compound appropriately called "filler," which can eventually be sanded smooth and painted. Joe has spent considerable effort researching and experimenting with various mixtures to get just the right properties, and, because he is a perfectionist, was still a little dissatisfied with his results 30 years into his part-time building career. Finally, in 1967, the proprietor of a one-man shop in Maine, across the Penobscot River from giant Old Town Canoe, shared with Seliga a recipe that Joe has tweaked to yield a filler that is perfectly satisfactory in every respect.

Unrolling a length of canvas from a roll that's kept under a bench along one wall, Joe traps one end of the folded duck in a homemade, tong-like, hinged wooden clamp that is secured by C-clamps.

(**above left**) One inside surface of the clamp features a ridge that fits into a matching slot on the other surface so that the canvas does not pull free when considerable force is exerted on it. The opening of the canvas "envelope" is faced down and the first clamped end is slid down over one end of the upside-down canoe.

(**above right**) After determining the exact length needed, Joe cuts the duck from the roll, completes the fold, and traps the other end in a similar clamp, already exerting some tension as he pulls it down over the other end.

(top opposite) The clamp at the left end is attached by a chain to a ringbolt anchored in the shop's foundation. The clamp at right is secured to the business end of a mechanical chain hoist, which is anchored to a ringbolt at the side of the shop. Beneath the canoe, Joe places two supports built the exact width of the canoe just inside the sawhorses. Slightly taller than the horses, they support the hull and allow the canvas to slide down as more tension is applied. Canoes that are curing, drying, or otherwise in progress are tucked into out-of-the-way spaces.

(bottom opposite) After more stretching with the hoist, Joe adds a second clamp that bolts together between the hinged clamps and the stems at each end of the canoe.

(left) Joe adds a final bit of tension.

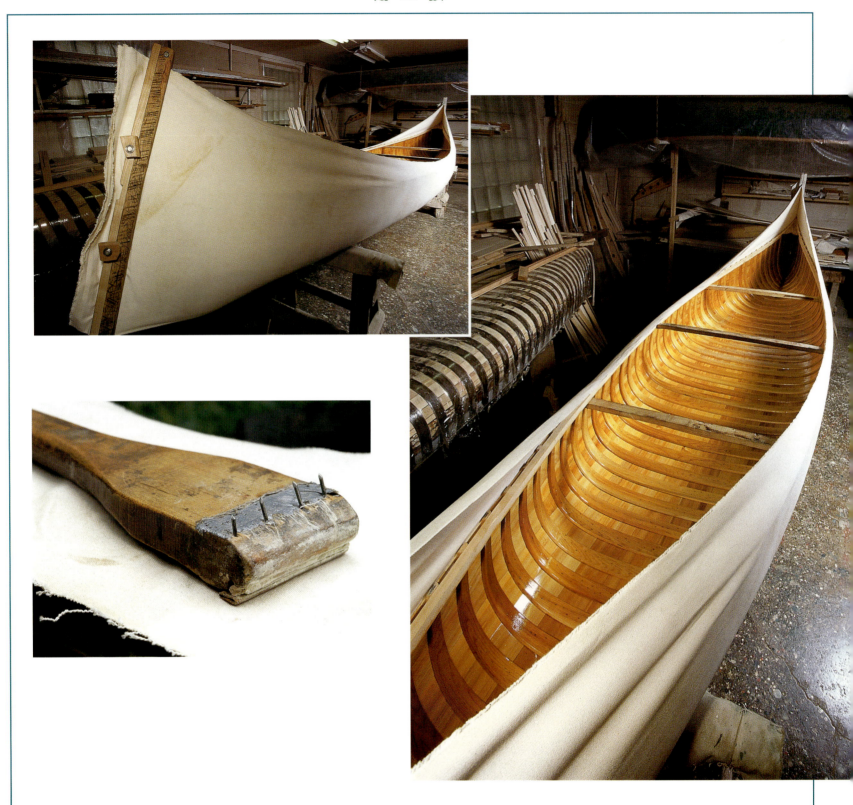

(top left opposite) The canvas may now be cut between the outer-hinged clamps and the inner bolted ones without losing any of the tension. This allows Joe to turn the canoe right side up on horses, better facilitating the pulling and stapling of the canvas to the canoe.

(bottom left opposite) This is Joe's homemade version of a carpet-stretching tool, which he uses to pull the canvas tightly across the hull and around the bow and stern.

(right opposite) The canoe inside its canvas cocoon before final pulling and stapling.

(above left) Using a metal guard to protect the gunwale and another version of a clawed stretching tool (handmade from half of an artist's canvas-stretching plier), Joe rocks the device inboard after catching the canvas to get the right tension.

(above right) Maintaining this tension, Joe uses an electric stapler to fire in a staple at each rib 1/8 inch below the top edge of the planking.

(above) Small dimples or folds above each staple at the planking line indicate just the right amount of tension. The rows of holes above are from the claws of the pliers.

(top right) Joe quickly runs the flame from a propane burner over the surface of the canvas, eliminating any fuzz or nap that makes smooth finishing later on more difficult.

(right) When Joe has pulled and stapled the canvas along the entire sheerline, he removes the end clamps and begins the overlapping seam at each end. At the bottom he has slit the excess fold back to the curve of the stem, where the canvas is taut against the curve. Then, using his carpet puller and starting at the top of the stem, he pulls one side tightly around and drives a couple of tacks into the stem face to secure it.

(above) Joe continues downward along this curve, pulling one side tight and tacking.

(above right) Nearing the bottom, he turns the canoe over and uses the smaller clawed plier to finish the first side, making an overlap at the end of the slit.

(right) Holding the first flap taut, Joe then trims it along the stem face with a utility knife.

(above) Joe applies a coat of canvas filler along the "under lap" for a sealer before pulling and tacking the second flap over the first.

(top right) Here, Joe has finished pulling the overlap, making certain it covers the first lap completely at the origin.

(right) Joe applies a thick first coat of his special weave filler to the raw canvas with a brush whose bristles have been cut short. This gives him a stiffer brush that works the filler deeper into the weave. The canoe is intentionally tilted for better visibility and to prevent the filler from running down along the canvas.

(left) Using a mitt made from the canvas off cuts, Joe rubs the filler until it is smooth and dry.

(bottom left) Joe applies a lighter second (and perhaps a third) coat using the same brush and a used canvas mitt with little "tooth" left, providing an even smoother surface than the first and, thus, the desired satiny finish. Once satisfied with the filling, Joe will let it dry for a couple of days. Then, he will lightly sand it to remove any fine fuzz that might have surfaced, and apply an extremely light coat of filler, again rubbing it smooth with an old mitt. The canoe will then be set aside for about a month while the filler cures.

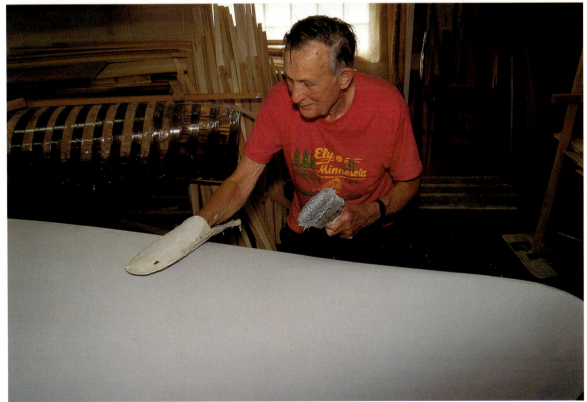

Outer Gunwales and Thwarts

There is not a lot Joe can do with a canoe while its filler cures, so he normally starts another canoe or perhaps finishes one that has cured sufficiently. He is not as insistent on this as he was in the past when working with Nora, but Joe clearly doesn't enjoy sitting around with nothing to do, and projects in the shop are always on his mind.

There are still a number of steps to complete after the filler has cured to the point that it is flinty when picked at with a thumbnail. Of all the filler's ingredients, the oils take the longest to dry, and even though the filler may appear hard enough to paint within a few days, the uncured oils would prevent the paint from adhering to the surface, causing trouble down the road. The last thing Joe wants to receive is a phone call from a customer reporting that the paint on a canoe purchased six months earlier is coming off in sheets.

Joe likes to get the final coats of spar varnish on the interior before the outer gunwales are installed. To get the glossy bright finish he insists upon, Joe applies at least four coats of varnish, often five. After the second, each subsequent coat requires a thorough light sanding of all surfaces, a tedious business when one considers the edges of the ribs, as well as their surfaces and the exposed planking between the ribs.

Joe also applies an initial coat or two of marine enamel paint on the filled canvas before gunwale installation. To prepare the cured surface Joe sands it thoroughly by hand with regular sandpaper. Not so many years ago, Joe used wetted silicon carbide sandpaper that created a slurry which didn't easily gum up the abrasive.

"Oh, you should've seen it," Joe remarks. "I'd have sludge all over the place. But it did a beautiful job, just as smooth as could be." Since he began using the light second filling mentioned above, he finds wet sanding no longer necessary—regular, dry paper is adequate for the job.

"It's just something I figured out over time," he explains. "You know, I'm always looking for an easier way to do something; as long as the results are the same."

Next, Joe spreads on a thin but even coat of paint with a brush. The following day the paint is dry enough for another light sanding and the application of the second coat.

The outer gunwales are usually mahogany but can be cherry or ash instead, depending on what stock is available and what the customer wants. Like the spruce inwales, the gunwales must have a sweep pre-bent into their ends, and so must be boiled and bent on the same jig used for the inwales. First, however, they must have a rabbet cut on the table saw, leaving a narrow lip along the top to fit over the planking.

In addition to making outer gunwales, Joe must shape and finish thwarts, and since the Boundary Waters are laced with almost as many portages as lakes, most of Joe's canoes are fitted with a center yoke, featuring substantial pads for a measure of comfort during this arduous work.

With the filler cured, it is safe to add any necessary coats of varnish on the interior to achieve a gleaming, durable finish.

The first and sometimes second coat of marine enamel paint is applied to the outside surface after the filler is sanded smooth. When the paint is dry, usually the next day, Joe runs a utility knife along the top edge of the canvas, slicing off the excess in preparation for outer gunwale installation.

(**left**) Joe runs the mahogany gunwales past a dado blade on the table saw to cut a beveled rabbet that complements the bevel running along the inwale and leaves a narrow lip along the top that will just cover the top edge of the planking and canvas.

(**bottom**) Two mahogany outer gunwales are taped back to back for boiling and bending. In addition to being rabbeted, each outer gunwale is thinned slightly in width toward the end. The bottoms of these gunwales will be varnished before installation.

(above) Joe begins clamping the gunwales amidships then works toward the ends, a method that allows less length to flop around and makes it easier to fit each end. They are pre-drilled for Number 8 bronze screws and countersunk just enough so the flat heads of the screws will be 1/16 inch or so below the surface.

(right) Joe uses a brace to install the screws. The clamps are removed as the rails are fastened in place. The cardboard shield protects the paint, and the small lengths of wood held across the tops of the gunwales by clamps help keep the inwales and outer gunwales level to one another.

(**above**) Joe uses a prop to hold the end of the new gunwale up in position. Even though it's pre-bent, there is enough tension remaining in the wood to make it difficult to hold and drill.

(**right**) Joe installs the final fastener at the end of the outer gunwale.

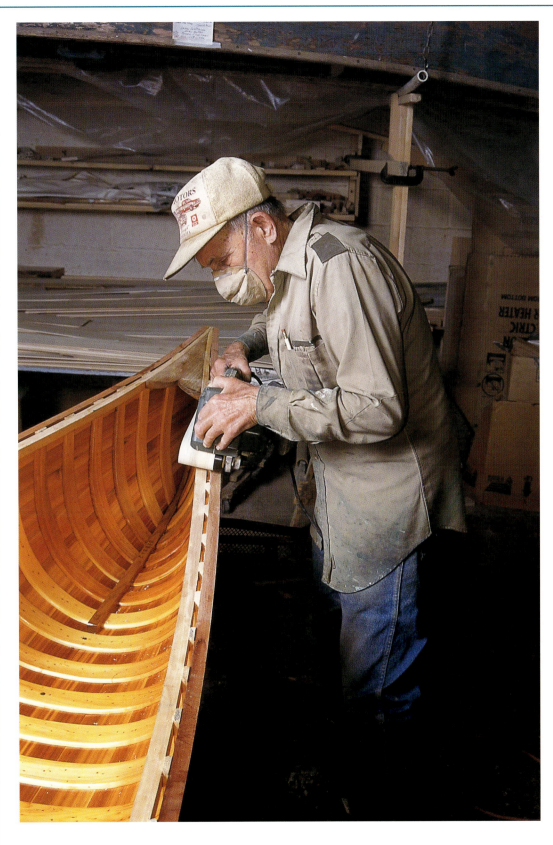

A belt sander run along the two gunwales sands the rib tops flush with the surface of the rails, creating an even and smooth surface.

(above) Joe also uses the belt sander to shape the sides of the outer gunwales alongside the decks and around the ends.

(right) Joe employs a handheld router to shape the edges of the gunwales outside and in.

(above left) The router bit removes the sharp corners of the two gunwales, making them more comfortable to handle, as well as more aesthetically pleasing. They will, however, still require a good deal of hand sanding before they are ready for finishing.

(middle left) Joe uses the dado head on his table saw and yet another jig to uniformly shape the 7/8-inch-thick thwarts.

(bottom left) The edges of the thwarts are rounded with the router. The square ends are left with sharp edges, a look Joe prefers when bolting them up against the bottom of the inwales.

(above right) The sanded thwarts are varnished before installation.

(top) The materials used to construct pads for Joe's contoured center thwart, or yoke, include a rectangular piece of dense, close-celled foam, a plywood base with inserts for the bolts that will secure the pads to the ash yoke itself, and a piece of leather-like vinyl.

(above) Joe pulls the vinyl tight with pliers and drives brass upholstery tacks with washers into the edges of the plywood.

(right) Joe makes a neat job of covering the ends of each pad.

(left) Once the pads are bolted to the finished yoke, the unit is ready to be clamped into place. The pads toe out slightly intentionally and extend a little forward on the yoke to accommodate the shape of the paddler's shoulders. Joe knows from experience exactly where the canoe will balance when hoisted by the paddler.

(above) Because of the torque that will be exerted on the joint when the canoe is lifted, Joe secures the yoke to the inwale with two machine screws on each end. The quarter thwarts, by contrast, are secured with a single bolt at each end.

Making and Installing Caned Seats, Varnishing, and Painting

Joe has always outfitted his canoes with natural cane seats, although for at least the past 30 years he has used commercially available woven cane mats as opposed to cane strands woven hole-to-hole around the frame of the seat. "I did that for years and years, and it's one heck of a job," he grimaces. "Five or six hours, at least, for one seat—I don't care who's doing it." The wooden seats on some Seliga canoes at Camp Widjiwagan, Joe points out, are repairs made by staffers over the years.

When Old Town began using pre-woven mats set into a groove machined around the seat frame, Seliga switched too. At first, he used his table saw to cut grooves into the individual seat pieces before assembly and finished up with a chisel. The square-cornered channels required Joe to miter-cut the rush spline into four pieces, which he felt was less than satisfactory from an aesthetic standpoint. "But you know, I couldn't for the life of me figure out how to router those round corners so I could use one piece of spline," he recalls.

In frustration, he began buying seats already caned from the Shaw & Tenney Company in Orono, Maine, makers of oars and paddles since 1854. Then, in 1981 at the Wooden Canoe Heritage Association's annual assembly in Orono, Seliga found himself sitting across the table from Paul Reagan, proprietor of Shaw and Tenney since 1975. "We got along real well and talked about all kinds of things," Joe says. "Paul is a heck of a nice guy. I told him I hadn't figured out how to rout those round corners." Reagan freely offered a solution and drew Joe a diagram.

"The minute I saw it, it made sense. It was one of those real simple things that are almost too simple," Joe recalls, looking back on the revelation. "Why I didn't think of that myself, I'll never know. I was so excited that when I got home I built about three dozen seats and tried it. And of course it worked fine. He didn't have to do that, you know, I wouldn't even've asked him."

Once the seats have been installed with 1/4-inch bronze carriage bolts, there is still work to be done before the customer can pick up his or her canoe, including the final painting, installing bronze stem bands on the ends, and applying the celebrated Seliga decal. Frequently, customers request keels along the bottoms of their canoes. These are made of ash and are 3/4 inch deep with their sides beveled so they are wider at the contact surface, which has a shallow hollow cut its entire length that Seliga fills with a sealant to prevent leaks. The ends of the keel are tapered at the ends in both height and width. The keel is then fastened to the canoe with bronze screws from the inside, through the ribs and into the harder keel. Tiny cone-shaped brass washers keep the screws from biting too deeply into the rib surfaces.

When a customer wants the protection of a keel, but plans to use his canoe frequently in fast water, Joe mills and installs a shallow shoe keel 2-1/2 inches wide and tapered at the ends. The shoe keel is barely 1/2 inch deep with rounded edges and is less prone to catch on ledges and other underwater obstacles than the standard version, making it less of a hazard in rapids.

Joe drills a pair of holes in a long seat-frame member to accommodate dowels.

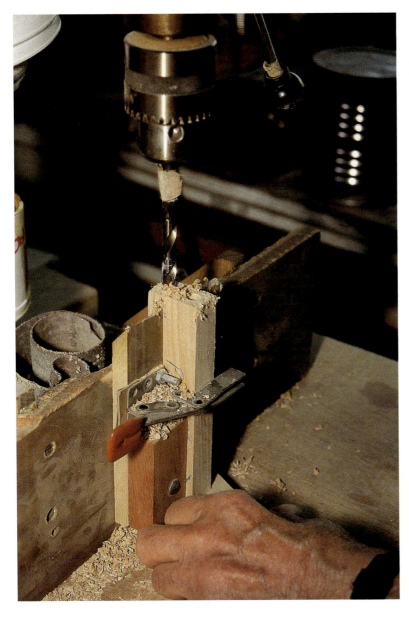

(left) Holes with the same spacing are bored into the ends of the shorter seat struts.

(above) The grooved dowels give the glue a better bonding surface.

(above) Joe assembles a seat frame using carpenter's glue.

(right) Here, Joe checks that the frame is square before clamping.

(above) With the seat frame dry, Joe routes its edges, then sands and varnishes it before routing the groove for the caning and spline.

(right) A pin combined with the inverted router bit allows Joe to achieve the groove's perfectly rounded corners.

(above) The cane mat has been soaking in warm water to make it pliable. Joe buys the pre-woven mats from commercial suppliers, but years ago wove the seats by hand.

(right) Joe positions the cane over the groove.

Covering the cane with a fitted board braced from above, Joe taps the ends into the groove with a blunted wooden wedge.

(above) Next, Joe uses a sharp chisel to trim the excess strands standing out from the groove.

(right) Joe cuts a beveled end on the rush spline that has also been soaking in water.

(left) After applying a bead of carpenter's glue into the groove, Joe taps the spline lightly into place.

(lower left) Finally, Joe seats the spline with a piece of hardwood and a few more raps of the hammer.

(left) Finished seats ready for installation.

(bottom) Having cut the seats to fit, Joe installs the bow seat just forward of the quarter thwart, and hung down with dowel spacers to lower the bow paddler's center of gravity.

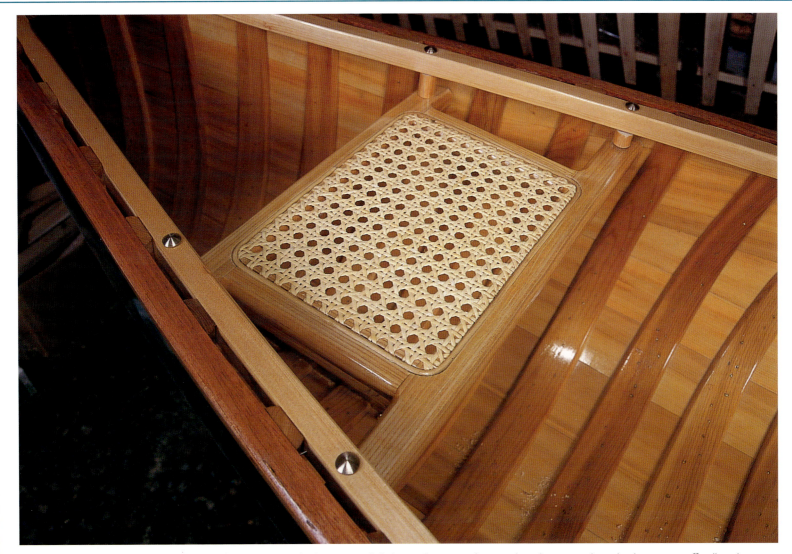

The position of the stern seat is nearer the end than the bow seat. It is hung down on shorter dowel spacers than the bow seat, affording the stern paddler a bit of visibility over his or her partner. Bronze carriage bolts are again the fasteners of choice.

(**above**) After lightly sanding the previous coat of paint and masking off the gunwale Joe uses a foam brush to expertly apply a final coat. Normally, he applies four or five coats of paint before he is satisfied with its smoothness and depth. Raising one side of the canoe gives Joe better light and a closer look at his work.

(**right**) Joe has painted canoes nearly every color imaginable, but the vast majority of his customers request a dark forest green.

When the paint is dry, Joe uses Number 4 screws to attach hollow-backed, bronze stem bands that will protect the ends of the canoe. Should the canoe have a keel, the stem band runs up the tapered end of the keel itself. Joe buys his stem bands from a supplier in Maine. For a period between 1965 and 1980 they were unavailable, so Joe, like other builders, made do with aluminum stem bands.

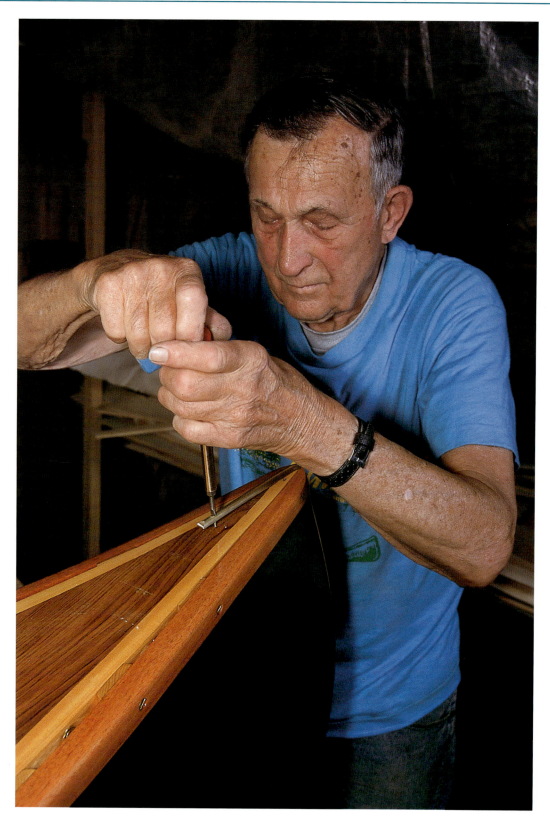

The upper end of the stem band is bent around the end of the gunwales and onto the deck, where Joe secures it.

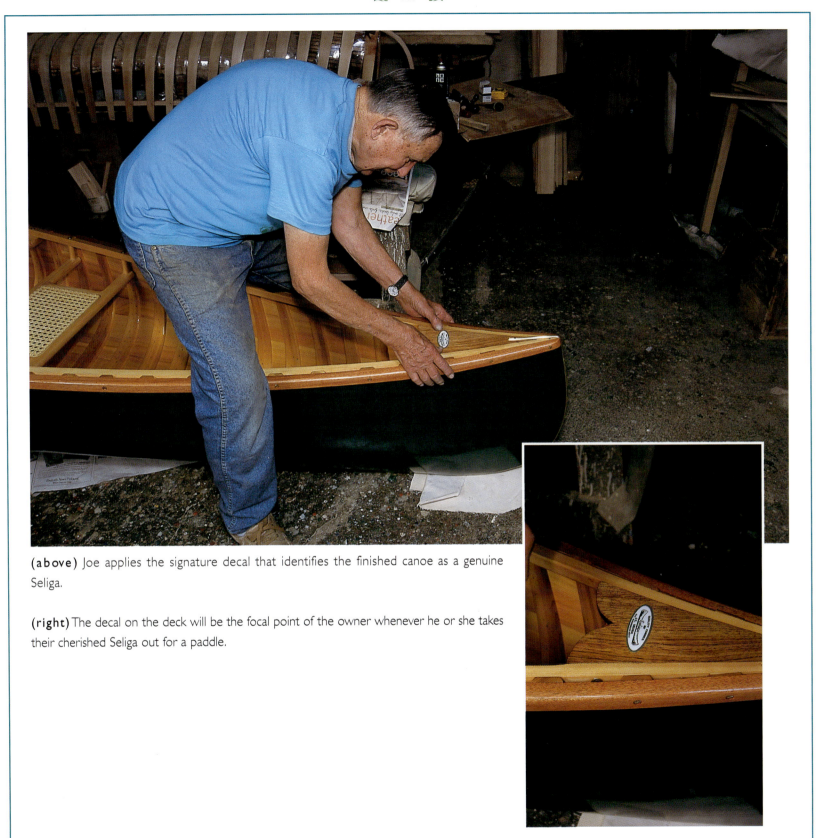

(above) Joe applies the signature decal that identifies the finished canoe as a genuine Seliga.

(right) The decal on the deck will be the focal point of the owner whenever he or she takes their cherished Seliga out for a paddle.

anatomy of a Seliga canoe:

Art from the Northwoods

Although wood-and-canvas canoes like Joe's are symmetrical, the front or forward end is designated the *bow*.

Also made of ash, the *center yoke* is shaped to accommodate the canoeist's neck during portaging and allow the two pads to rest on the shoulders. The yoke pads are made of dense, closed-cell foam covered in vinyl.

At each end of a Seliga canoe, a black cherry *deck* joins the ends together. Joe has also used ash and mahogany for this purpose. E. H. Gerrish of Bangor, Maine, the first wood-and-canvas-canoe manufacturer leaned toward heart-shaped decks and perhaps provided the inspiration for B. N. Morris, who used this shape almost exclusively and had a profound influence on many builders, including Joe.

Each quarter of the canoe includes a cross-piece called a *thwart* made of ash to help the canoe hold its shape.

The width of the canoe at the center, or *midships*, is called the *beam*. On a Seliga canoe, the beam is 36 inches. The distance between the top of the gunwale and the bottom inside at midships is the canoe's *depth*—13 inches on a Seliga canoe.

The side of the canoe can either flare out at the gunwale or curve in. An inward curve is referred to as a *tumblehome*. In modifying the design of the 18-foot Morris, Joe retained the tumblehome, but relaxed it just a bit.

The seats in a Seliga canoe are made of ash frames filled with mats of natural cane. The stern seat is farther from the center than is the bow seat. Both seats are bolted to the inwales with bronze carriage bolts and dropped down a bit with dowel spacers to lower the paddler's center of gravity. The stern seat is mounted higher than the bow to afford the stern paddler greater visibility.

Viewed from the end, the contrasting gunwales bring the canoe's shape to life.

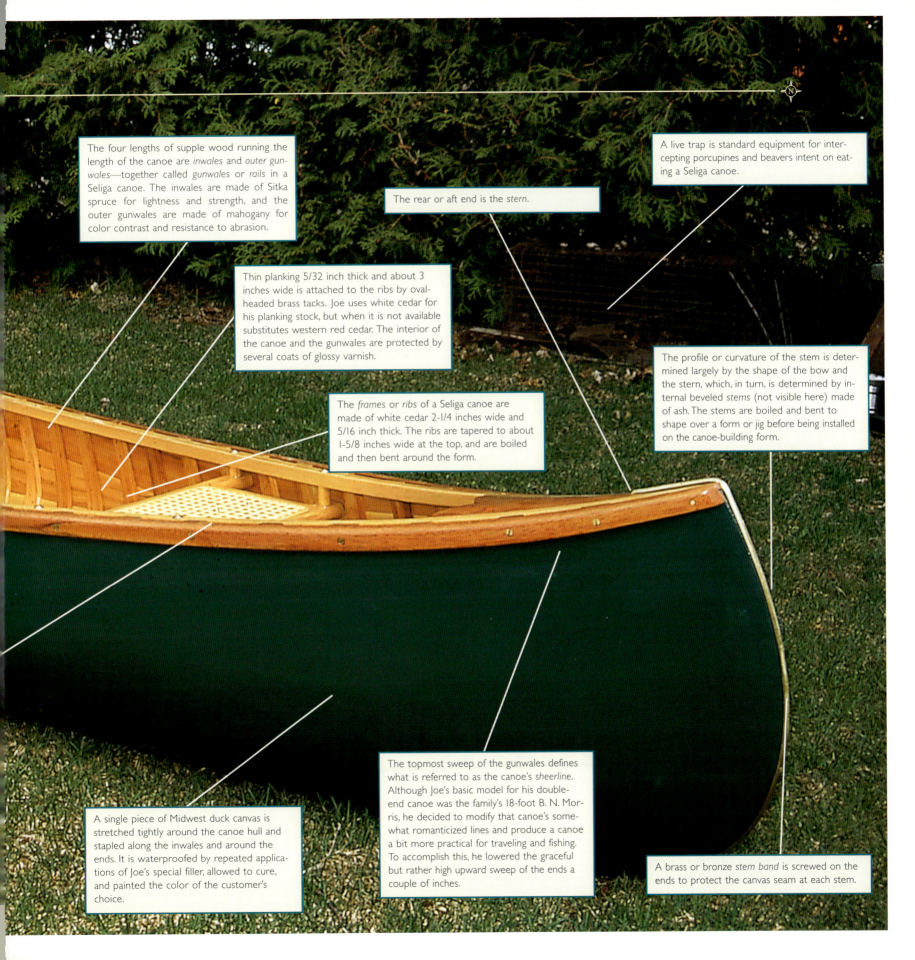

The Magic Continues

Dan and Jane Badger of Duluth, Minnesota, take delivery of Seliga canoe 01 654 9—their second—on March 18, 2002. Dan was a camper at Camp Menogyn during the summers of 1975 through 1979. *Courtesy of Badger Family*

The day after St. Patrick's Day in 2002, Dan Badger and his family are driving north to Ely from their home outside Duluth, Minnesota. It is an exciting day for Dan, his wife Jane, and their two children, Ellen, 8, and Karl, 4. A few days before, they'd received a telephone call from Joe Seliga announcing that the canoe Dan had ordered for Jane a few years back was finished and ready to be picked up. A Seliga canoe is not an unknown quantity for the Badgers. In 1993, the couple took delivery of a beautiful green Seliga that has kept the pair in touch with their pasts and secured a direction for their future, at least recreationally. Dan and Jane are both avid canoeists, and they hope Ellen and Karl pick up on their enthusiasm and follow suit.

Dan was a camper at Camp Menogyn on the Gunflint Trail during the summers of 1975 through 1979. According to Dan, there are still a dozen or so Seliga canoes in the camp's canoe shed.

"The guides got to paddle the Seligas when I was at Menogyn," Dan recalls. "It wasn't until my fourth summer, when I did a 21-day trip in north-central Ontario, that I got to be in charge of one." The experience was memorable enough for Dan to order his own Seliga canoe as soon as it was feasible—the Badgers picked it up a few months before the shop fire of 1994.

Joe greets the Badgers when they pull up beside his house at the appointed hour. His daughter JoAnn, her husband Jan, and a few other family members are up visiting. The Badgers are no strangers to Joe, having visited him at least once a year during their frequent trips to the Boundary Waters. He starts right in ribbing Jane.

"Red," he muses. "Why did you have to have it red? Don't you know canoes are supposed to be green?"

She is flabbergasted by the work before her—Seliga canoe 01 654 9—and for a couple of minutes can only repeat, "Oh, it's so beautiful, I can't believe it. It's so beautiful." She's snapped out of her trance by Joe. "Look at this," he says, producing a printout of the Seliga canoe records, comprehensively and accurately compiled by Dan Lindberg. In it is a pie chart indicating the colors that Seliga has painted his Seliga canoes over the years. "Look at this, Jane," he repeats. "Seventy-five percent of my canoes have been painted green. But green wasn't good enough for you, was it?" he jokes.

The jokes and stories continue until the canoe is tied to the car and ready for the trip to its new home. When Dan asks what paint to buy so he can keep the canoe up, Joe pulls out a can of Valspar "Racing Red."

"See, with this on your canoe, Jane, your canoe will be a lot faster than Dan's," Joe kids.

"That's great," Dan quickly retorts. "That way, she can make camp and do all the portaging."

"I never thought of that!" Joe laughs.

On their way home, the Badgers are refreshed by their visit with Joe Seliga, and pleased as can be with Jane's new canoe. Dan can't believe his good fortune. A couple of years back, when he discreetly inquired of Joe if it were still possible to order a canoe, Joe had told him, "Well, these days, I'm making canoes just for the family, mostly. But you know, Dan, I'll put your name on the 'good list' and if things work out maybe you'll be getting a call from me."

Joe would take no money up front. So when the call came in early winter that Jane's canoe was under construction, Dan and Jane were a happy pair, indeed. When the canoe is launched in the spring, the living legacy of the Seliga canoe will once more be strengthened by paddlers who know firsthand how special these works of northwoods art really are.

After the Badgers and Joe's families have concluded their brief visit and driven off to their homes, Joe walks out to the shop. He disposes of a pile of shavings by using it as kindling in the barrel wood stove. Once it's burning brightly, he closes the damper and walks over to a pile of cedar boards drying below the blower of the small furnace that keeps the shop above freezing. Joe smiles, thinking to himself, "This is really fine cedar. Time to rip out a set of ribs and get something started on the old form."

He grins to himself. "Spring's just round the corner, and I don't want to be stuck in here when there're walleyes to catch."

index

B. N. Morris Boat & Canoe Company, 26, 30
B. N. Morris (models), 17, 22–26, 30, 36, 49, 89, 123
    15-footer, 23, 30, 37, 44–45, 48, 79
    18-footer, 22–23, 25, 30, 33–34, 36, 89, 164
    Model D, 30
Badger, Dan, 166–167
Badger, Jane, 166–167
Big Moose Lake, 22
Binger, Bob, 45, 49, 71, 73
Bissonet, Millie, 12
Blueberry Arts Festival, 16
Boat shows, 60
Boundary Waters Canoe Area Wilderness (BWCAW), 8, 12–13, 24, 42, 74, 140, 167
Bourquin, Jeanne, 62–63, 69
Bowermaster, Jon, 20
Boy Scouts of America, 50
Brandenburg, Jim, 11, 19
Brandenburg Gallery, 11
Braun, Mike, 63
Britton's (Brit's) Café, 12, 68
Building the Seliga canoe, 80–165
    Caned seats (making and installing), 150–163
    Canvassing, 130–139
    Decks (making and installing), 123–129
    Form (setting up), 89–94
    Hull, 114–129
        Completing, 114–122
        Sanding, 123–129
    Outer gunwales and thwarts, 140–149
    Planking, 104–113
    Ribs (bending), 95–103
    Stock (preparing), 80–88
    Varnishing and painting, 150–163
Burntside Dam, 30
Burntside Lake, 24, 30, 45, 56, 71, 74
Camp DuNord, 74
Camp Menogyn, 59, 167
Camp Sherwood, 73
Camp Widjiwagan ("Widji"), 8, 45, 48, 59, 63, 67, 70–79, 150
    Canoe shop, 76, 78–79
Canadian Border Outfitters, 17
Captive Mining Corporation, 55
Carlton, Guy, 26
Cary, "Jackpine" Bob, 9, 17, 19, 68
Chandler Mine, 15

"Charlie's (Charlie) guide," 11, 45, 50, 59, 61, 66
Charles L. Sommers Wilderness Canoe Base, 11, 50, 62
Cherne, Les, 44
Chestnut brothers, 123
Chestnut canoes, 48, 59
Chocolate Moose restaurant, 16, 19
Civil Works Administration (CWA), 32, 35
Civilian Conservation Corps (CCC), 32, 35
Cook, Sam, 8
Echo, The (newspaper), 17
Echo Trail, 22, 31, 33, 66, 73
Ely (history), 14, 15
Fiberglass (Joe's experiments with), 52–53
Fillers, 48, 59
Fire (1994), 62–63
Form (Joe's first), 38
Gerrish, E. H., 26, 89, 123, 164
Grant, Walter, 26
Great Depression, 31, 35, 44
Gunflint Trail, 59
Hanson, Harlan, 39
Herter's, 52
Holmberg, Patti, 19
"Hoover Days," 31
International Wolf Center, 19, 21, 74
Iron ore, 35
Iron Range, 14, 44
Jeffery, Wilbur, 73–74
Kennebec Canoe Company, 26, 36
Kirby, Julian, 71, 74
Kolbe, Joe, 41
Kranz, Tom, 74, 77
Krogar, Eleanor (Seliga, Nora), 31–32
Kuralt, Charles, 17
Laurentian Divide, 14
Lindberg, Dan, 167
Litchfield, Dan, 65
Lucky Boy, 63
Luehrs, Armin "Whitey", 73
Mackenzie, Alexander, 73
Mattson, Ray, 39
Mech, David, 74
Mesabi Range, 14
Metrodome (boat show), 60, 65
Miner's Lake, 14–15
Moose River, 73
Morris, B.N. (Bert), 26, 36, 123, 164
National Geographic, 11
Nilsen, Christopher, 43
Nilsen, Jan, 43, 68

Nina Moose River, 22–23, 33
Nora and Joe Seliga Wood Canoe Endowment, 77
"Nora's Canoe," 70, 77, 79
Northern Grounds Café, 17
Northern Tier High Adventures, 11, 50
Old Town Canoe, 26, 36, 38, 48, 58, 123, 130, 150
Oliver Mining, 35
Olson, Sigurd, 17, 24, 29
    Fraser Bill, The 24
    Listening Point, 24
    Listening Point Foundation, The, 24
    Singing Wilderness, The, 24
    Wilderness Society, 24
Penobscot River, 26
Pickands-Mather's, 44
Pioneer Mine, 11, 15
Piragis, Nancy, 19
Piragis, Steve, 19
Piragis International Expeditions, 19
Piragis Northwoods Outfitters, 19
Plymouth Youth Center, 55, 63
Prezioso, Michael, 76–77, 79
Quetico Provincial Park, 42, 70, 73
Reserve Mining, 58, 60
Retirement, 60
Rice Lake, 30
Richards, Allison, 64
Richards, Tim, 68
Roundy, Melvin, 123
Schurke, Paul, 17, 20, 21
    North to the Pole, 21
    Wilderness Inquiry, 21
Schurke, Susan, 19
Seliga, Albert, 27
Seliga, Ann (Joe's grandmother), 22, 27
Seliga, Ann (Joe's sister), 27, 40, 68
Seliga, Anna, 22, 27, 68
Seliga, Daniel, 27, 44
Seliga, Dorothy, 27
Seliga, Ethel, 27, 68
Seliga, Helen, 27
Seliga, JoAnn (Nilsen), 37, 44, 67–68
Seliga, John, 27, 68
Seliga, Margaret, 27, 68
Seliga, Nancy (Richard Seliga's wife), 67
Seliga, Nancy (Richards), 48, 67–68
Seliga, Michel, 15, 27
Seliga, Nora (Krogar, Eleanor), 32, 35, 37, 44, 51–53, 55–56, 61–64, 66–67, 69, 95–96
Seliga, Richard, 32–33, 35, 49, 51, 68

Seliga, Rose, 27
Seliga, Rudolph "Rudy," 27, 68
Seliga, Stephen, 15, 27, 33, 36, 68
Seliga, Stephen, Jr., 27, 35–36
Seliga canoes (models)
    17-footer, 50, 104
        Anatomy, 164–165
    18-footer with "V" stern, 50
    Fiberglass, 52–53
    "Fisherman" (16-foot square stern), 35, 38, 40–41, 43, 48
    "Voyager" (18-foot), 71
Shagawa Lake, 14–15, 22, 27, 30, 34, 63
Shaw & Tenney Company, 150
Sheridan Street, 13, 19
Smith, Joe, 63, 75
Sommers, Charles, 50
Sommers Canoe Base, 8, 39–45, 48, 59
Steger Mukluk store, 15, 21
Steger, Will, 17, 20–21
    Crossing Antarctica, 20
    Saving the Earth, 20
Superior National Forest, 35
Thomas, Homer, 36
Thompson, Rolfe, 74
Thurlow, Rollin, 26, 123
Timoney, Kevin, 54
Trezona Trail, 14–15
U.S. Steel Corporation, 29–30, 35
Valspar "Racing Red," 167
Veazie, Maine, 26, 59
Vermilion Range, 14
Voyageur Winter Carnival, 16
Walberg, Eric, 41
WELY radio, 16–17
Wheat, Ben, 41
White, E. M., 17, 123
White Iron Lake, 30
White Street house, 28–29, 33, 35, 38
Whiteside Park, 16
Wintergreen Designs, 19, 21
Wintergreen Lodge, 21
Wooden Canoe Heritage Association (WCHA), 54, 57, 60, 150
World War II, 44
Works Progress Administration (WPA), 32, 35
Zenith Mine, 15, 49, 55